Part 1 Financial Planning, Performance, and Analytics: Certified Management Accountant CMA

Azhar ul Haque Sario

Copyright

First Printing, 2025

Azhar.sario@hotmail.co.uk

ORCID: https://orcid.org/0009-0004-8629-830X
LinkedIn: https://www.linkedin.com/in/azharulhaquesario/

Disclaimer: This book is free from AI use. The cover was designed in Canva.

Copyright Disclaimer: This book is an independently produced study resource. The author, Azhar ul Haque Sario, has no affiliation with the Institute of Management Accountants (IMA) or the certification board. All references to "Certified Management Accountant" and "CMA" are used under nominative fair use for educational purposes to describe the subject matter of the book.

Contents

External Financial Reporting Decisions (15% - Levels A, B, and C)

Financial statements

The Balance Sheet

In the past, the Balance Sheet was often viewed as a "snapshot"—a static photo. In 2026, think of it as a live dashboard.

For a Management Accountant, this document answers the two most primal questions of business survival:

What resources do we control? (The engines of future cash flow).

Who has a claim on those resources? (The creditors and the owners).

The 2026 syllabus adds a layer of complexity: Sustainability and Digitization. You aren't just counting cash anymore; you are valuing volatile crypto assets, estimating environmental cleanup costs (ESG), and predicting credit losses with AI models.

2. The Golden Rule: The Accounting Equation

Everything rests on one immutable law of physics in the financial universe. You cannot create value out of thin air; every resource must be funded by someone.
Assets=Liabilities+Equity

Think of this as "The Stuff" vs. "The Funding."

Assets (The Uses): "We bought a factory."

Liabilities (The Sources - External): "We took a loan to buy the factory."

Equity (The Sources - Internal): "The owners put in cash to buy the factory."

2026 Reality Check: An asset is only an asset if it provides future economic benefit. A server that cannot run modern AI algorithms is not an asset, regardless of what you paid for it. It's an expense waiting to happen.

3. The New Frontiers of 2026

The classic definitions of assets and liabilities have evolved. Here are the three "Game Changers" you must master for the exam.

A. Digital Assets (The Crypto Shift)

This is the biggest verifiable change. Historically, crypto was treated like a broken machine—you recorded losses, but never gains.

The Old Way: Cost minus Impairment.

The 2026 Way (Fair Value): If you hold Bitcoin and the price skyrockets, your Balance Sheet immediately shows that value, and the gain hits your Net Income. It is volatility in real-time.

B. The "Invisible" Debt (Leases)

Companies used to hide rental agreements in the footnotes to make their debt look lower. That loophole is closed (ASC 842 / IFRS 16).

The Reality: If you rent a fleet of trucks, you have a Right-of-Use Asset and a massive Lease Liability. This hurts debt ratios but reflects reality.

C. The ESG Liability

If a company pollutes today with a promise to clean it up in 2035, that obligation is a liability now. You must estimate the present value of that future cleanup and book it.
4. Case Study: A Year in the Life of "Nebula Dynamics"

Let's apply this to the real world. Meet Nebula Dynamics, a robotics startup operating in 2026.

The Context:

Industry: Robotics & AI.

Strategy: High growth, tech-heavy, holding crypto reserves.

Status: First year of operations (Jan 1 – Dec 31, 2026).

The "Live" Log (Transactions)

We need to process the chaos of a business year into an orderly statement.

Event Type	The Story	The Financial Impact
Founding	Owners invest cash.	Cash ↑ \$600k / Equity ↑ \$600k
Leverage	Bank loan taken (5% interest).	Cash ↑ \$200k / Liability ↑ \$200k
Capex	Bought high-tech servers.	Cash ↓ \$180k / PPE (Asset) ↑ \$180k
Inventory	Bought robot parts on credit.	Inventory ↑ \$150k / Accts Payable ↑ \$150k
Crypto Bet	Bought 2 Bitcoin @ \$20k each.	Cash ↓ \$40k / Digital Asset ↑ \$40k
Sales	Sold robots. Half cash, half credit.	Cash ↑ \$200k / AR ↑ \$200k / Revenue \$400k
Operations	Paid bills and suppliers.	Cash ↓ \$200k total / Exp & Liab ↓

The Strategic Adjustments (Year-End)

This is where the Accountant adds value over the Bookkeeper. We must adjust for time and risk.

Crypto Mark-to-Market: The Bitcoin bought for \$40k is now worth \$70k. We must record this \$30k gain.

CECL (Credit Losses): We predict \$5k of our customers won't pay. We reduce the asset value now, not later.

Depreciation: The servers are wearing out. We expense \$36k of their value.

5. The Solution: Nebula Dynamics Balance Sheet

Below is the "Anchor of Truth" for Nebula Dynamics as of Dec 31, 2026.

Nebula Dynamics, Inc. Statement of Financial Position

ASSETS (What we have)	Amount	Notes
Current Assets		
Cash & Cash Equivalents	$580,000	High liquidity; safe.
Accounts Receivable (Net)	$195,000	Adjusted for the $5k predicted loss.
Inventory	$40,000	What's left on the shelves.
Total Current Assets	$815,000	
Non-Current Assets		
Digital Assets (Crypto)	$70,000	Valued at Market Price (Level 1 Fair Value).
Property, Plant & Equip (Net)	$144,000	Cost minus $36k depreciation.
Total Non-Current Assets	$214,000	
TOTAL ASSETS	$1,029,000	

LIABILITIES & EQUITY (Who funded it)	Amount	Notes
Current Liabilities		
Accounts Payable	$70,000	What we still owe suppliers.
Interest Payable	$10,000	Accrued interest on the loan.
Total Current Liabilities	$80,000	
Non-Current Liabilities		
Long-Term Bank Loan	$200,000	Due in 2031.
Total Liabilities	$280,000	
Equity		
Common Stock	$600,000	Initial Investment.
Retained Earnings	$149,000	Includes the $30k Crypto Gain.
Total Equity	$749,000	

TOTAL LIAB & EQUITY $1,029,000 Balanced.

6. The Strategic Readout

As a CMA, you don't just build the spreadsheet; you read the tea leaves. What does this sheet tell us about Nebula Dynamics?

Extreme Liquidity: The company has $815k in liquid assets to pay just $80k in bills. This is incredibly safe, but potentially inefficient. Strategic Question: Why is so much cash sitting idle? Should we invest more in R&D?

The Crypto Boost: The Retained Earnings are healthy ($149k), but roughly 20% of that profit came from the Bitcoin price surge, not operations. Risk Note: This profit is volatile. If Bitcoin crashes next month, Equity will shrink.

Low Leverage: The company is mostly funded by owners ($749k) rather than debt ($280k). This gives them financial flexibility to borrow more if they need to expand rapidly in 2027.

The Income Statement (CMA 2026)

Introduction: The Movie vs. The Poster

Think of a company like a blockbuster movie. The Balance Sheet is the movie poster. It's a frozen moment in time—the glamorous shot of the heroes looking strong. It tells you who is in the movie (Assets) and who paid for the costumes (Liabilities/Equity).

The Income Statement? That represents the actual movie. It is the footage. It captures the action, the drama, the explosions, and the plot twists over a period of time.

For the 2026 CMA exam, the IMA doesn't want you to be a film critic who just memorizes the cast list. They want you to be the Director. They want you to understand how the story is told, how to edit out the noise, and how to use modern tech to predict the sequel.

1. The Plot: Did We Win or Lose?

At its heart, the Income Statement answers one brutally honest question: Did we actually accomplish anything this year?

The script is simple:
Net Income=(Revenue−Expenses)+(Gains−Losses)

But here is the trap for new players: Net Income is just the main plot. There is a spin-off called Comprehensive Income.

Net Income: Goes to Retained Earnings. This is the money we can re-invest or buy pizza with.

Other Comprehensive Income (OCI): This is the "behind the scenes" footage (like currency adjustments). It skips the Income Statement and goes straight to Equity. Don't confuse the main plot with the behind-the-scenes features.

2. The Format: Single-Step vs. Multi-Step

Imagine trying to watch a movie where all the scenes are shuffled randomly. That is a Single-Step Income Statement. It dumps all revenues in one bucket and all expenses in another. It's technically correct, but it's terrible storytelling.

The CMA exam (and Wall Street) prefers the Multi-Step Format. This organizes the movie into "Acts," allowing you to judge performance at different levels:

Act I: Gross Profit (The Product).

Revenue minus Cost of Goods Sold (COGS).

The Story: Is our actual product profitable? If you sell lemonade for $1.00 but the lemons cost $1.50, your movie ends here. No amount of accounting magic can save you.

Act II: Operating Income / EBIT (The Business).

Gross Profit minus Operating Expenses (SG&A).

The Story: The product is good, but is the company functional? Are we spending too much on the CEO's private jet or the marketing budget? This measures management's skill.

Act III: Net Income (The Bottom Line).

After interest and taxes.

The Story: This is what's left for the shareholders after the government and the banks take their cut.

3. Revenue Recognition: The "Don't Count Your Chickens" Rule

In the old days, you booked revenue when the check cleared. In 2026 (under ASC 606), you book revenue when you fulfill a promise.

Think of it like a gym membership. If "TechFlow 2026" sells a $1,200 annual subscription on January 1st, they have $1,200 in cash, but zero revenue. Why? Because they haven't done anything yet.

The 5-Step Model is your script for when to clap:

The Handshake: Identify the contract.

The Promises: What are we delivering? (Software? Support? Training?)

The Price Tag: How much is the whole deal worth?

The Split: Assign a price to each promise.

Action: Recognize revenue only as you do the work (e.g., $100/month).

The Vibe: Revenue is earned, not just collected.

4. Expenses: The Law of Karma (Matching Principle)

In accounting, every action has an equal and opposite reaction. You cannot claim the glory of a sale without admitting the pain of the cost to get there.

Product Costs (COGS): These are attached to the product like a shadow. You buy leather to make shoes. You cannot expense that leather until the shoes are sold. Until then, the cost sits on the Balance Sheet in "Inventory" limbo.

Period Costs (SG&A): These are attached to the calendar. The rent for the factory is due whether you make 1 shoe or 1,000. Expense it immediately.

A Note on Depreciation: Depreciation isn't about valuation; it's about fairness. If you buy a $100k robot that lasts 10 years, it's unfair to dump a $100k expense on Year 1 and $0 on Year 2. You spread the pain out so it matches the years the robot helps you make money.
5. Plot Twists: The "Irregular" Items

Every now and then, something weird happens. As a CMA, you need to tell the audience (investors) whether this is a recurring villain or a one-time cameo.
A. Discontinued Operations (The Break-Up)

If Ford decides to stop making sedans to focus on trucks, that is a strategic shift. We handle this like a breakup.

We move the results of the "Sedan Division" to the very bottom of the page.

We report it Net of Tax.

Why? So investors can look at the top of the page and see the "Continuing Operations"—the future of the company—without the noise of the ex-partner.

B. The Death of "Extraordinary Items"

There used to be a category for "Extraordinary Items" (like a volcano erupting in Nebraska). Update for 2026: This category is dead. GAAP eliminated it. Now, even weird events are part of "Continuing Operations."

6. EPS: Slicing the Pizza

Earnings Per Share (EPS) is the most famous number in finance. Imagine Net Income is a pizza. EPS tells you how much pizza each share of stock gets.

Basic EPS: The pizza divided by the people currently at the table.

Diluted EPS: The "Paranoid Scenario." This asks: "What if everyone who has a coupon (stock options) or a VIP pass (convertible bonds) showed up right now to eat?"

More people = smaller slices. This is Dilution. You must report the worst-case scenario so investors aren't blindsided.

7. GAAP vs. IFRS: The Cultural Differences

Since you are taking a global exam, you need to know the local customs.

Feature	US GAAP (USA)	IFRS (International)
Inventory	Allows LIFO (Last-In, First-Out). We like it because it lowers taxes when prices rise.	LIFO is banned. It makes no physical sense.

Mistakes If you write down the value of inventory, it stays down. No take-backs. If the value recovers, you can reverse the write-down. Optimism is allowed.
Format Flexible. No strict list of required line items. Strict. Must list finance costs and tax expense explicitly.

8. The 2026 Edge: You Are Not a Calculator

Here is the reality of the 2026 exam: The robots have won the math war. Software can calculate the Gross Margin in 0.002 seconds. The exam doesn't test if you can add; it tests if you can analyze.

Don't just calculate variance; explain it. Why did Gross Margin drop? Was it higher material costs, or did we offer too many discounts?

Continuous Accounting: The books don't close at the end of the month anymore; they close every second. Your job is to monitor the live stream.

Predictive Analytics: Use the historical data to draw a line into the future. Regression analysis isn't just for statisticians; it's for CFOs.

Final Takeaway: The Storyteller

When you sit for Part 1 of the CMA in 2026, don't just look for the right number. Look for the story.

If a company has high Net Income but plummeting Operating Income, they might be selling off assets to hide a failing business model. If they have huge Revenue but no Cash Flow, they might be "stuffing the channel" with fake sales.

You are the doctor, the director, and the detective. The Income Statement is your evidence. Read it carefully.

The Narrative of Numbers: Orion Robotics FY2026

To: The Board of Directors & Strategic Planning Committee From: Corporate Controller Subject: The Story Behind the Statement – Transitioning from Playthings to Powerhouses

We often treat the Income Statement as a scorecard—did we win or lose? But for fiscal year 2026, Orion Robotics' Income Statement is not just a scorecard; it is a manifesto.

We are witnessing a metamorphosis. We have shed the skin of a toy company to reveal an industrial automation titan. A standard single-step statement would blur this reality. By using the Multi-Step Format, we are carefully dissecting our anatomy to show investors exactly which muscles are strong and which limbs we had to amputate to survive.

Here is the narrative of our year, decoded.
I. The Top Line: Reality vs. Invoices

Net Sales: $4,300,000

In accounting, as in life, it's not about what you ask for; it's about what you keep.

We invoiced $4.5 million in Gross Sales. However, the "Top Line" that matters is the $4.3 million Net Sales. Why the gap? The $200,000 in Returns & Allowances.

The Controller's Pulse Check: In the toy business, returns meant a kid didn't like the color. In industrial robotics, a return means a gyroscope failed in a warehouse. This number is our "Quality Control Metric."

The "Matching Principle" in Action: We booked this deduction now. We don't wait for the client to ship the defective unit back in January 2027. We take the hit in 2026 because that's when the revenue was recognized. It is painful, but it is honest.

II. The Core Engine: Gross Profit

Gross Profit: $2,200,000

This is where the rubber meets the road—or rather, where the lithium meets the carbon fiber.

After stripping away the direct costs of manufacturing (COGS)—the batteries, the assembly labor, the factory electricity—we are left with $2.2 million.
Gross Margin=4,300,0002,200,000≈51.1%

Why this excites me: A 51% margin is the hallmark of a premium technology player. If we were selling commodities, this would be 20%. This number tells the Board that we have Pricing Power. Our clients aren't buying a drone; they are buying an efficiency solution, and they are willing to pay a premium for it.

III. The "Middle Line": Operating Expenses

Total OpEx: $1,550,000

If COGS is the cost of the product, Operating Expenses are the cost of time and talent.

Selling ($450k): The fuel for our growth engine (commissions and ads).

Admin ($800k): The infrastructure. I am flagging this. When admin costs outpace sales growth, companies become sluggish. We need to watch this "overhead bloat" in 2027.

R&D ($300k) – The Gamble:

The GAAP Reality Check: Under US GAAP, we expensed this $300k immediately. We took the hit to our profit today for technology that might not pay off until 2028.

If we were in Europe using IFRS, we might have "capitalized" this, hiding the cost on the Balance Sheet. But we are taking the conservative route. We are telling investors: "We are spending cash now to invent the future."

IV. The Verdict: Operating Income (EBIT)

Operating Income: $650,000

This is the most critical number on the page.

Forget the taxes (government mandated) and the interest (bank mandated). This number asks: Is the core business of making industrial drones actually viable?

The answer is a resounding YES. We generated $650k in pure operational profit. This covers our interest payments ten times over. The heart of Orion is healthy.

V. Noise Below the Line

Interest & Gains

We separate these to keep the "story" clean.

Interest Expense ($60k): The cost of leverage.

Gain on Equipment ($40k): We sold an old machine. This is "lucky money." We isolated this so analysts don't accidentally assume we will sell a machine for a profit every single year.

VI. The Tax Logic: Intraperiod Allocation

Income from Continuing Ops (After-Tax): $472,500

Tax allocation sounds complex, but the philosophy is simple: Let the tax follow the income.

We calculated the tax only on the robotic operations first.
630,000×0.25=157,500 (Tax Expense)

This leaves us with $472,500. This is the number analysts should plug into their spreadsheets for 2027 projections. It represents the sustainable, recurring earnings of Orion Robotics.

VII. Discontinued Operations: Cutting the Anchor

Net Loss from Discontinued Ops: ($75,000)

This line item represents our past: The Toy Division. We shut it down. It cost us money to close the doors, resulting in a pre-tax loss of $100,000.

The Silver Lining (Tax Benefit): Because Orion is profitable, the IRS allows us to use that $100k loss to offset our gains.

- The Loss: ($100,000)
- The Tax Savings (25%): +$25,000
- The Net Hit: ($75,000)

By isolating this at the bottom of the statement, we are signaling to the market: "This $75k loss is a scar, not a wound. It is healed, it is gone, and it will not bleed into 2027."

VIII. The Headline: Earnings Per Share (EPS)

Wall Street loves a single number, but a single number lies.

- Net Income EPS ($0.80): The official bottom line.
- Continuing Ops EPS ($0.95): The real value.

Strategic Narrative: If we only show the $0.80, the market undervalues us. We must direct their eyes to the $0.95. This metric proves that for every share an investor owns, our actual business generated 95 cents of profit. The 15-cent drag from the toy division is history.

Controller's Summary

The Fiscal Year 2026 Multi-Step Income Statement is a declaration of intent.

- We are efficient: 51% Gross Margins prove it.
- We are conservative: Expensing R&D proves it.
- We are focused: Disposing of the toy division proves it.

Orion Robotics is no longer playing games. We are building the industrial future, and our financials finally reflect that reality.

The Autopsy of a Fiscal Year: Orion Robotics (2026)

An Income Statement isn't just a spreadsheet; it is a story of triumphs, failures, expensive lessons, and the literal cost of doing business. For Orion Robotics, 2026 was a year of shedding dead weight and doubling down on heavy industry.

Here is how the chaos of the real world translated into the bottom line.
Part 1: The Narrative Feed (The "Real" Story)

Before we get to the clean final numbers, we have to look at the messy reality of the last 12 months.

1. The Hero Product (Gross Sales) The "Atlas-X" Industrial Drone was the star of the show. We didn't just sell units; we moved heavy metal. We shipped 150 units to logistics giants like Amazon and FedEx. At $30k a pop, the revenue engine was roaring.

The Scoreboard: $4,500,000 in Gross Sales.

2. The Reality Check (Returns & Allowances) Hardware is hard. A batch of gyroscopes failed calibration, forcing five clients to return their units for a full refund ($150k). Another client found scratches on the chassis; rather than ship them back, we cut them a deal and knocked $50k off the price. It hurts, but it keeps the relationship alive.

The Hit: $200,000 lost to quality control issues.

3. The Guts of the Machine (COGS) You can't build a drone out of thin air. It takes lithium, carbon fiber, and highly skilled labor. We burned through $1.2M in raw materials and paid our assembly team $600k. Keeping the factory lights on and the machines running cost another $300k.

The Cost: $2,100,000 to build what we sold.

4. Keeping the Lights On (OpEx) This is the "overhead" beast. We had to pay the salespeople to close those Amazon deals ($450k), pay the executives and lawyers to

steer the ship ($800k), and fund the "mad scientists" in the back room working on the Next-Gen AI prototype ($300k).

The Burn: $1,550,000 in Operating Expenses.

5. The Garage Sale & The Bank (Other Items) We had to pay the bank $60k in interest on our startup loans. However, we found a silver lining: an old hydraulic press gathering dust in the back. Book value said it was worth $10k; we managed to sell it for $50k.

The Result: A net cost of $20,000 (Interest outweighing the gain).

6. Cutting the Dead Limb (Discontinued Ops) It was time to admit defeat on the "Robo-Pup" toy division. It was a distraction. We shut it down, paid the severance, and broke the lease. It cost us $100k upfront, but it stops the bleeding for next year.

The Loss: $100,000 (Pre-tax).

7. The Tax Man The government takes their slice: 25%. However, the tax code works both ways—while they tax our profits, they also give us a tax break on that massive loss from the Robo-Pup division.

Part 2: The Financial Portrait (Multi-Step Income Statement)

When we organize that narrative into "Good Form," it provides a clear cascade from top-line hype to bottom-line reality.

Orion Robotics Inc. Income Statement For the Year Ended December 31, 2026

Item Detail Subtotal Total
Sales Revenue
Gross Sales (The "Atlas-X" Revenue) $4,500,000
Less: Sales Returns & Allowances ($200,000)
Net Sales $4,300,000

Cost of Goods Sold (COGS) ($2,100,000)
Gross Profit (What we made on the hardware) $2,200,000

Operating Expenses
Selling Expenses (Commissions/Ads) $450,000
General & Admin (Salaries/Rent) $800,000
R&D (The Future Tech) $300,000
Total Operating Expenses ($1,550,000)
Operating Income (EBIT) $650,000

Other Revenues, Gains, Expenses & Losses
Interest Expense ($60,000)
Gain on Sale of Equipment $40,000
Total Other Items ($20,000)

Income from Continuing Operations (Pre-Tax) $630,000
Income Tax Expense (25%) ($157,500)
Income from Continuing Operations (After-Tax) $472,500

Discontinued Operations
Loss from "Robo-Pup" Division (Pre-Tax) ($100,000)

Less: Income Tax Benefit (25%) $25,000
Net Loss on Discontinued Operations ($75,000)

Net Income	$397,500

Part 3: The Shareholder's Takeaway (EPS)

What does this mean for the people holding the stock? Based on 500,000 shares, here is the breakdown of value per ticket.

Metric	The Story	EPS Value
Continuing Operations	If we only look at the healthy part of the business (The Atlas-X drones), we are profitable.	$0.95
Discontinued Ops	The failure of the "Robo-Pup" division dragged down the share value, but it's a one-time hit.	($0.15)
Net Income	The final walk-away profit per share.	$0.80

Summary Analysis

Orion Robotics is fundamentally healthy. The core business (Continuing Operations) is generating nearly a dollar per share. The final Net Income ($397,500) looks lower strictly because the company made the brave decision to amputate a failing limb (The Toy Division). Next year, without the "Robo-Pup" losses, the bottom line should instantly spring back up.

Mastering Statement of changes in equity & Statement of cash flows

Welcome to the future of the CMA.

If this were 2015, I'd tell you to memorize formats and punch numbers into a calculator until your fingers cramped. But it's 2026. The bots are doing the data entry. The AI is handling the reconciliations.

So, what is left for you? The Story.

Financial statements are no longer just compliance documents; they are the narrative arc of a company's life. The Balance Sheet is a selfie—a static moment in time. But the Statement of Changes in Equity and the Statement of Cash Flows? They are the movie. They show motion, drama, decisions, and consequences.

Let's decode the movie.
Part 1: The Corporate Diary (Statement of Changes in Equity)

Think of Equity not as a math problem, but as the Company's DNA. It answers one question for the shareholders: "Is my slice of the pie getting bigger because the company is winning, or just because you shifted numbers around?"

In the 2026 landscape, Equity is a living ecosystem with four distinct "buckets."

1. Share Capital: The "Foundation"

This is the handshake deal. The "Par Value." It's the historic legal capital.

The 2026 Twist: Watch for "Dual-Class Structures." Founders love keeping control while selling equity. You might see Class A and Class B shares where the dollar value is the same, but the power dynamic is totally different.

The Trap: Treasury Stock. If the company buys its own shares back, don't be fooled—this isn't an asset. It's a "contra-equity." It's the company saying, "We don't need this capital right now," and shrinking the pie.

2. APIC (Additional Paid-In Capital): The "Street Cred"

Nobody pays "Par Value" anymore. If a share has a sticker price of $1, but the market pays $50, that extra $49 is the APIC. It represents the premium investors are willing to pay for your potential.

3. Retained Earnings: The "War Chest"

This is the company's internal fuel engine.

The Formula: Beginning RE+Net Income−Dividends=Ending RE

The Human Insight: High Retained Earnings means the company believes it can grow your money better than you can. Low Retained Earnings (high dividends) means the company is saying, "Here, you take the cash; we're out of big ideas." In the high-rate environment of the mid-2020s, companies hoarding Retained Earnings are avoiding expensive bank debt.

4. AOCI (Accumulated Other Comprehensive Income): The "Waiting Room"

This is the most misunderstood bucket. Think of AOCI as a purgatory for gains and losses. These are real economic changes—like the value of your European subsidiary crashing because the Euro fell, or your bond portfolio spiking in value—but they haven't been "realized" by a sale yet. They aren't allowed into the VIP section (Net Income) yet. They wait here in the lobby.

The "Pizza Slicer" Analogy (Stock Splits vs. Dividends)

The CMA exam loves to trick you here.

Stock Split: You take a large pizza and cut it into 16 slices instead of 8. Do you have more pizza? No. You just have smaller slices. Total Equity impact: $0.

Stock Dividend: You take a slice of pizza from the "Retained Earnings" box and move it to the "Share Capital" box. You still have the same amount of pizza on the table; it's just categorized differently. Total Equity impact: $0.

Part 2: The Truth Serum (Statement of Cash Flows)

If the Income Statement is a company's Instagram (filtered, curated, accrual-based), the Cash Flow Statement is its Checking Account (raw, honest, brutal).

Profits are an opinion. Cash is a fact.
The Three Buckets of Truth

Operating (The Hustle): Can this company pay its light bill?

The 2026 Shift: Under IFRS 18, we are getting strict. We are purging "investment income" (like interest received) out of this section to find the true operating profit. If this number is negative while Net Income is positive, run. It means they are booking sales but not collecting cash.

Investing (The Future): Is the company planting seeds or eating them?

The ESG Angle: Look for "Green CapEx." This is cash bleeding out now to retrofit factories for a carbon-neutral 2030. It hurts cash flow today but saves the company tomorrow.

Financing (The Credit Card): Who is funding the party?

The Golden Rule: Paying Interest is usually Operating (the cost of doing business), but paying back the Principal is Financing (clearing the debt). Don't mix them up.

The Methodology: The "Reverse Engineering" (Indirect Method)

Most companies use the Indirect Method. It's a reconciliation logic puzzle.

Depreciation: We add it back. Why? because we subtracted it to find Net Income, but we never actually wrote a check for it. It's a "phantom expense."

Working Capital Logic:

If Inventory goes UP, Cash goes DOWN. (You spent money to buy those widgets sitting on the shelf).

If Accounts Payable goes UP, Cash goes UP. (You hoarded cash by not paying your bills yet).

Part 3: The 2026 Synthesis (The "Sherlock Holmes" Moment)

The robot can generate the report. You, the 2026 CMA, need to diagnose the patient. You need to spot the patterns that don't make sense.

The "Danger Zone" Pattern:

Net Income: ↑ (Looks great!)

Operating Cash Flow: ↓ (Disaster!)

The Diagnosis: The company is stuffing the channel. They are forcing products onto customers who aren't paying (bloated Accounts Receivable) just to hit a sales target. The profits are fake; the cash crisis is real.

The "Fake Wealth" Pattern:

Total Equity: ↑ (Looks rich!)

Retained Earnings: – (Flat)

AOCI: ↑ (Huge spike)

The Diagnosis: The company didn't actually make money selling products. They just got lucky because the currency exchange rate moved in their favor, or their bond portfolio inflated. This is "paper wealth," not operational success.

To: 2026 CMA Candidate From: Your Strategic Partner Subject: De-coding the Matrix: How Business Moves Become Financial Lines
The Art of Financial Storytelling

Most textbooks treat accounting like a calculator exercise. It isn't. It is the language of business strategy. When you sit for the CMA exam, you aren't just a bookkeeper; you are an interpreter.

Today, we are looking at Apex Sustainable Energy Corp. Think of this company not as a spreadsheet, but as a living, breathing entity that is hungry for growth. We are going to translate two massive strategic moves into the rigid grammar of US GAAP.

Phase 1: The Strategic Moves (The "Why" and "What")

Before we touch a ledger, we need to understand what the Board of Directors is actually doing.

1. The War Chest Expansion (Transaction A)

The Date: June 15, 2026 The Move: Apex wants to dominate the solar market. To do that, they need cash—lots of it. They don't want a loan; they want partners.

The Action: They issue 50,000 shares.

The Valuation: Investors are so bullish they pay $25.00 for a share that has a legal "par value" of only $1.00.

The Sweetener: To keep current owners from revolting over the dilution, the Board tosses them a bone: a $0.50 dividend per share on the new total (150,000 shares).

The Human Translation: Apex just convinced the market that they are worth 25x their paper value. They are trading ownership for a massive influx of liquidity.

2. The Strategic Pivot (Transaction B)

The Date: September 10, 2026 The Move: Apex is cleaning house. Old wind tech is out; efficiency is in.

The Action: They sell an old machine for $80,000.

The Math: It cost $100k and had $40k in wear-and-tear (depreciation). Book value was $60k.

The Result: They made a $20,000 "paper profit" (Gain).

The Follow-up: They take $50,000 of that cash and kill a high-interest long-term debt.

The Human Translation: They are liquidating a legacy asset to clean up their balance sheet (reduce debt). This makes them leaner and more attractive to future investors.

Phase 2: The Translation (The Statements)

Now, let's watch where these numbers land. This is where the CMA exam tests your ability to categorize wealth.

1. The Statement of Changes in Equity (The Wealth Story)

This statement tracks the net worth of the shareholders. Pay attention to the "Par" vs. "Premium" split.

Components	Share Capital (Par)	Add. Paid-In Capital (The Premium)	Retained Earnings (The Savings)	AOCI (The Noise)	Total Equity
Start of Year	$100,000	$500,000	$850,000	($20,000)	$1,430,000
Net Income	-	-	$320,000	-	$320,000
Currency Adj.	-	-	-	$15,000	$15,000
Stock Issuance	$50,000	$1,200,000	-	-	$1,250,000
Dividends	-	-	($75,000)	-	($75,000)
End of Year	$150,000	$1,700,000	$1,095,000	($5,000)	$2,940,000

Analyst Insight: Look at the APIC column. It jumped by $1.2 million, while Share Capital only moved $50k. This tells you the "Par Value" is legally required nonsense. The real value of this company lies in the premium investors are willing to pay. Also, note that the Dividend came out of Retained Earnings—you can't pay dividends from Share Capital.

2. The Statement of Cash Flows (The Truth Serum)

This is the most critical document for a CMA. Net Income ($320k) is an opinion; Cash Flow is a fact. We use the Indirect Method to peel back the layers.

Operating Activities (Running the Business)

Net Income: $320,000

Add: Depreciation (Non-cash expense): +$45,000

Less: Gain on Sale of Equipment: ($20,000)

The "Why": This is the trickiest part. The $20k gain is already inside Net Income. But selling equipment isn't "Operating"—it's "Investing." We have to remove the ghost so we don't count it twice.

Changes in Working Capital (AP/AR): ($5,000)

Net Operating Cash: $340,000

Investing Activities (Building the Future)

Sale of Equipment: +$80,000

Note: Here is where we show the actual cash received from the machine.

Purchase of New Machinery: ($200,000)

Net Investing Cash: ($120,000)

Financing Activities (Funding the Dream)

Stock Issuance: +$1,250,000

Note: The biggest number on the page. This is the "War Chest."

Debt Repayment: ($50,000)

Dividends Paid: ($75,000)

Net Financing Cash: $1,125,000

The Bottom Line

Cash Increase: $1,345,000

Ending Cash: $1,495,000

Phase 3: The "Sherlock Holmes" Conclusion

If you hand these statements to a computer, it checks if the debits equal the credits. If you hand them to a CMA, they see the narrative.

The Narrative of 2026: Apex is not relying on its day-to-day operations to grow. While operations are healthy ($340k), the company has fundamentally altered its DNA through Financing.

The Signal: They are sitting on nearly $1.5 million in cash (up from $150k).

The Intent: You don't dilute ownership and raise $1.25 million just to let it sit in a bank account. You also don't pay off long-term debt unless you want to clean up your credit rating.

The Prediction: Apex is preparing for a Major Acquisition or a massive infrastructure build in 2027. They have loaded the gun; next year, they fire it.

CMA Exam Takeaway: When you see a "Gain on Sale," your reflex must be: Remove from Operating, Add full proceeds to Investing. When you see a "Stock Issuance," your reflex must be: Split the Par and the Premium.

The numbers tell a story. Make sure you're reading it.

Consolidated statements and Integrated reporting

Welcome to the future. If you are reading this in preparation for 2026, you likely realize that the era of the "Bean Counter" is dead. The stereotype of the accountant sitting in a basement, isolated, tallying debits and credits? Gone.

The 2026 CMA is an Architect of Value. You don't just record history; you design the future. You are fluent in two languages: the precise, rigid language of Consolidation, and the fluid, interconnected language of Integrated Reporting.

Here is how we humanize the ledger.

Part I: The Fiction of Truth (Consolidated Financial Statements)

Accounting is often called the "language of business," but in Consolidation, it becomes a form of legal fiction. We create a "lie" to tell the truth.

Imagine a family. The father owns a bakery; the daughter owns a delivery van. Legally, they are separate people. But economically? They are one unit. If the father pays the daughter $50 to deliver bread, the family hasn't actually made money. They just moved cash from the kitchen counter to the glove box.

Consolidated Statements represent the act of erasing the walls between the rooms to show the size of the whole house.

1. The Power Dynamic (The "Control" Test)

In the old days, we counted shares. "You own 51%? You're the boss." In 2026, we look at human dynamics. We look for Control.

Think of Control as a "Three-Legged Stool" (IFRS 10 / ASC 810). If you kick one leg out, the stool falls, and you do not consolidate.

Power: Do you hold the steering wheel? (Can you fire the CEO? Set the budget?)

Returns: Do you feel the bumps in the road? (Do you get the dividends or suffer the losses?)

Linkage: Does turning the wheel actually move the car? (Can you use your power to influence your returns?)

The Human Element: You can own 40% of a company but still be the "Puppet Master" if you appoint the Board. If you pull the strings, you own the show.

2. The Great Eraser (Eliminations)

This is where the Alchemist works. To see the true picture, we must delete the "internal noise."

The Investment Mirror: You cannot invest in yourself. We wipe the Parent's "Investment" asset against the Subsidiary's "Equity." Poof. Gone. What remains is usually Goodwill—the premium you paid for the subsidiary's "mojo" (reputation, vibe, legacy).

The "Left Pocket" Rule: If "AutoCorp" sells an engine to "TireCo" for a profit, but the engine is still sitting in the garage... that profit is fake. It's a hallucination. We must eliminate the Revenue, the Cost, and the phantom Profit in inventory.

3. The Guests at the Table (NCI)

Sometimes, you own the house, but you rent out a room. You control the company (80%), but strangers own the rest (20%). These strangers are the Non-Controlling Interest (NCI).

We bring 100% of the assets onto the table because we control them.

But at dessert, we have to admit: "We made $1 million, but this slice ($200k) belongs to the minority partners." It is a humble nod to the other owners.

Part II: The Ghost in the Machine (Integrated Reporting)

If Consolidation is the body (the hard assets), Integrated Reporting (<IR>) is the soul.

The 80/20 Flip: In 1975, 80% of the S&P 500's value was physical (factories, trucks). Today, 90% of value is intangible. It is brand love, data algorithms, and employee brilliance. A Balance Sheet cannot see these things. If you fire your best engineers to save cash, your Balance Sheet looks great today, but your company is dead tomorrow. fixes this blindness. It views the company as a living organism (an Octopus) that consumes six types of "fuel" (Capitals) to create value.

The Six Capitals: The Lifeblood of Business

To be a CMA in 2026, you must understand how these capitals bleed into one another.

The Capital	The "Human" Definition	The Risk/Opportunity
Financial	The Blood. Cash, equity, debt.	Without it, the organism dies immediately. But having it doesn't guarantee a future.

Manufactured	The Skeleton. Buildings, IT, fleets.
	Are you investing in electric trucks (Green) or old diesel guzzlers (obsolete)?
Intellectual	The Brain. Patents, code, secrets.	Example: A pharma company is nothing without the patent. The pill press is cheap; the formula is priceless.
Human	The Muscle. Skills, loyalty, drive. The Critical Metric: High turnover kills value. You can't put "Employee Morale" on a balance sheet, but if it drops, revenue follows.
Social	The Heart. Reputation, trust, community.	A mine with gold (Natural) is worthless if the local town protests and shuts it down (Social).
Natural	The Oxygen. Air, water, minerals.	Business consumes nature. If you consume it faster than it renews, you act as a parasite, not a partner.

The "Connectivity" Strategy

This is the ultimate soft skill. You must explain the Trade-Offs.

The Diversity Example: Let's look at the intersection of Human and Financial capital using real data.

The Action: A company invests heavily in diversity recruitment and inclusive leadership training.

The Short-Term: Financial Capital decreases (Training is expensive).

The Long-Term: Human and Social Capital skyrocket.

The Payoff: According to McKinsey's Diversity Wins report, companies in the top quartile for ethnic and cultural diversity on executive teams were 36% more likely to have above-average profitability than those in the fourth quartile.

The Integrated Report connects these dots: "We spent cash today (Financial -) to build a diverse team (Human +), because diverse teams innovate better (Intellectual +), leading to higher future margins (Financial +)."

Summary: Your Role in 2026

The computer can calculate the elimination of an intercompany receivable. The AI can balance the Consolidated Statement.

But the AI cannot tell the story.

Only you can look at a pile of cash and explain how converting it into "Employee Training" or "Cleaner Water" will save the company five years from now.

Module 1 gives you the rules to count the wealth we have today.

Module 2 gives you the vision to create the wealth of tomorrow.

Part 1: The "One Big Happy Family" Rule (Consolidated Financial Statements)

Imagine you have a left pocket and a right pocket. If you move a $20 bill from the left to the right, are you richer? No. You just moved the money.

Consolidation is essentially the accounting police ensuring companies don't pretend they got richer just by moving money between their own pockets (Subsidiaries) and their wallet (Parent).

The Story: Apex Motors & The Battery Hype

The Setup:

The Big Boss: Apex Motors (The Parent).

The New Kid: VoltBattery Inc. (The Subsidiary).

The Deal: On Jan 1, 2026, Apex buys control (80%) of Volt.

The "Fake" Business (Intercompany Trade): Throughout the year, Volt makes battery packs and sells them to Apex.

Volt says: "Woohoo! I made $200,000 in sales!"

Apex says: "I bought $200,000 in inventory!"

The Problem: To the outside world, this transaction doesn't exist. It's just Apex moving batteries from its factory floor to its warehouse.

The "Backstage" Cleanup (The Eliminations)

Before we show the investors the final numbers, we have to run "Elimination Entries." Think of this as Photoshop—we are editing out the internal mess to show a clean final image.

1. The "Ghost Profit" Exorcism (Unrealized Profit)

This is where most students trip up.

Volt sold batteries to Apex for $200k.

It cost Volt $150k to make them.

Volt thinks it made a $50k profit.

However, by year-end, Apex still has half those batteries sitting in the warehouse. They haven't been sold to a real customer (a driver) yet.

Since 50% of the batteries are stuck inside the company, 50% of that profit is fake.

The Math:
$50,000 Total Profit×50%=$25,000 Fake Profit

The Fix: We have to deflate the inventory value by $25,000 so the Balance Sheet shows what the batteries actually cost to make, not the inflated price Volt charged Apex.
2. The "Double Vision" Correction (Intercompany Sales)

If we simply added Apex's books to Volt's books, we'd show $200,000 of revenue that never left the family. The Fix: We delete the entire sale.

Debit Sales $200k / Credit COGS $200k.

Poof. It never happened.

The Single Entity View (The "Why")

When you look at the Consolidated Balance Sheet, notice that the line item "Investment in Volt" ($800,000) has vanished.

Why? Because you can't invest in yourself. instead, that line is replaced by Volt's actual stuff—their cash, their machines, and their inventory (minus the fake profit). We are presenting Apex and Volt not as two handshaking partners, but as one giant economic organism.

Part 2: The "3D Chess" of Accounting

(Integrated Reporting)

Traditional accounting is like reading a score in a sports game. It tells you who won (Profit) and by how much (Cash Flow).

Integrated Reporting is the highlight reel. It tells you how they won, if the players are injured (Human Capital), and if the stadium is still standing (Natural Capital).

The Story: BlueRiver's Expensive Water

The Crisis: BlueRiver Textiles is running out of water, and the townspeople hate them for polluting the river. The Move: They drop $15 Million on a "Zero-Liquid Discharge" plant.

The Accountant vs. The Value Creator

If you look at this transaction through two different lenses, you see two different realities.

Lens A: The Traditional Accountant (2D View)

Journal Entry: Debit Asset (Plant), Credit Cash ($15M).

Analysis: "Ouch. We just lost significant liquidity. Free Cash Flow is tanking. Shareholders might panic about the dividend."

Lens B: The Integrated Reporter (3D View) This is where the magic happens. We admit we lost money (Financial Capital), but we explain what we bought with it. We traded one type of capital for three others.

The Capital Swap Narrative

In the 2026 Integrated Report, we don't apologize for the expense; we frame it as a strategic trade.

We spent Gold (Financial Capital): Down $15M.

To buy Security (Natural Capital): We aren't sucking the river dry anymore. We own our own recycled water loop.

To buy Trust (Social Capital): The protests stop. The government grants us a 20-year permit. We have a "License to Operate."

To buy Brainpower (Intellectual Capital): Our engineers had to learn complex filtration tech. They are now smarter and more valuable assets.

The Bottom Line for the CMA

When you write this report, you are connecting the dots.

"We didn't just buy a machine. We bought immunity from the upcoming drought."

The $15M wasn't a cost; it was insurance on **$40M of future revenue** that would have been lost if the factory shut down due to water shortages.
Summary: The "Human" Takeaway

Consolidation is about honesty: Don't count money you moved between your own pockets.

Integrated Reporting is about storytelling: Don't just list the cost; explain the value gained in reputation, resilience, and knowledge.

Recognition, measurement, and valuation

The Balance Sheet as a Storyboard: Cracking the 2026 CMA Code

Let's be honest: for decades, accounting was viewed as the art of recording history. It was a rearview mirror. But as we approach the 2026 CMA exam, that mirror has shattered. The new syllabus isn't asking you to be a historian; it's asking you to be a futurist.

In the 2026 landscape, driven by predictive analytics and intense ESG scrutiny, the balance sheet is no longer a static snapshot. It is a living, breathing ecosystem. When we talk about valuation now, we aren't just asking "What did this cost?" We are asking, "What is this actually worth in a world dominated by AI, climate change, and market volatility?"

Here is your human-centric, strategic guide to mastering Valuation for the modern CMA.
Part I: Assets – The Arsenal

Think of assets not just as "things we own," but as the tools we use to wage war in the marketplace. The 2026 exam demands you know which tools are sharp (liquid) and which are rusting (impaired).
1. The Cash Reality Check

Cash is king, but in 2026, the king has rules. You can't just lump everything into a bank account.

The "Ring-Fence" Trap: If you have cash sitting in an account legally reserved for paying off a bond (a sinking fund), you cannot call that "Cash and Equivalents." It's

Restricted Cash. It's like having money in a glass case—you can see it, but you can't touch it for operations.

2. Receivables: The "Will They Pay?" Algorithm

In the old days, we guessed how many customers wouldn't pay. In 2026, we use data.

The Predictive Shift: Imagine you are the CFO of "TechFlow." You don't just guess a 5% default rate. Your AI model analyzes payment behaviors and tells you, with terrifying accuracy, that 5% of your clients are about to ghost you.

The Valuation: You record the $1,000,000 owed to you, but you immediately strip away the fantasy. You report the Net Realizable Value (NRV) of $950,000. That $50,000 loss is the price of doing business.

3. Inventory: The Flow of Goods

This is where the tax strategy game is played.

FIFO (First-In, First-Out): Imagine a grocery store. You sell the milk that expires soonest. In inflation, this makes your profits look huge (old cheap costs vs. new high prices), but Uncle Sam takes a bigger bite in taxes.

LIFO (Last-In, First-Out): US GAAP only. You sell the "newest" expensive stuff first. Your profits look lower, but you save on taxes. It's a shield against inflation.

4. The Crypto Curveball & Strategic Investments

The 2026 syllabus finally caught up with the blockchain.

The Crypto Update: It used to be that if Bitcoin crashed, you booked a loss, but if it soared, you couldn't book a gain until you sold. Not anymore. Now, crypto is measured at Fair Value. If Bitcoin jumps, your Net Income jumps. Volatility is now front and center.

The "Why" Matters: Are you day-trading (Trading Securities) or holding for safety (Available-for-Sale)? The former hits your Profit/Loss immediately; the latter sits quietly in Equity (OCI) until you sell.

5. PPE & The "Stranded Asset" Nightmare

Here is where ESG (Environmental, Social, and Governance) gets real.

The Scenario: You own a perfectly good coal-fired power plant. It works. But, new 2026 environmental laws make it illegal to operate without expensive filters you can't afford.

The Impairment: Physically, the asset is fine. Legally, it is dead. This is a Stranded Asset. You must write its value down, potentially to zero, immediately. The CMA wants you to spot these "hidden" risks.

Part II: Liabilities – The Promises

Liabilities are often viewed negatively, but they are actually just "reversed assets"—they are the leverage we use to grow.

1. The Time-Travel of Bonds

A bond is simply a time machine. You are borrowing from the future.

The Discount/Premium Dance: If the market wants 7% interest, but your bond only pays 5%, nobody wants to pay full price for it. You have to put it on sale (Discount).

The Book Value: Over the life of the bond, that discounted price slowly floats up (amortizes) until it hits the face value at maturity. You are essentially paying extra interest expense every year to make up for that initial "sale price."

2. Leases: No More Secrets

Companies used to hide massive rental obligations in the footnotes. ASC 842 and IFRS 16 turned the lights on.

The New Normal: If you lease a fleet of trucks, that is now a liability on your books. It blows up your Debt-to-Equity ratio. As a CMA, you need to explain to the Board why the company suddenly looks "riskier" even though nothing operationally changed.

3. The AI Warranty

Stop guessing.

The Tech Edge: Instead of setting aside a flat 2% for warranties, modern companies use sensor data. If the sensors say 1.4% of engines will fail, you value your liability at exactly that cost. It is precision accounting.

Part III: Equity – The Soul of the Business

Assets−Liabilities=Equity

It looks like a math equation, but it's actually a trust score.

1. Treasury Stock: The Power Move

Why would a company buy its own stock?

The Signal: It's a flex. It tells the market, "We believe in ourselves so much, we're investing in us."

The Mechanics: It reduces total equity. It's a contra-account. But by reducing the number of shares available, it boosts Earnings Per Share (EPS), often making the remaining shareholders very happy.

2. Stock Options: The Golden Handcuffs

In the modern tech economy, we often pay people with dreams (options) rather than cash.

The Cost: Even though no cash leaves the bank, there is a cost. We use models (like Black-Scholes) to calculate the fair value of that "dream" on the day we grant it, and we expense it over the time the employee has to work to earn it (vesting). It lowers Net Income today to secure talent for tomorrow.

The Final Verdict: The "Whole-Ledger" Mindset

To crush the 2026 CMA, you have to stop acting like a calculator. The computer can calculate depreciation. The computer can track daily crypto fluctuations.

Your job is the narrative.

When you see LIFO: Think "Tax Strategy."

When you see Impairment: Think "ESG Risk."

When you see Leases: Think "Transparency."

You are the translator between the cold hard numbers and the strategic reality of the business. Go tell that story.

The Story of Profit: CMA Part 1 (2026 Focus)

Accounting isn't just about counting beans; it's about telling the story of those beans. Did we actually earn them? Did we keep them? And how do we explain that story to the world?

For the 2026 CMA exam, you need to think less like a calculator and more like a narrator. We are going to break down Revenue Recognition, Income Measurement, and the "Atlantic Divide" (GAAP vs. IFRS) by looking at the why and the how.

D. Revenue Recognition: The 5-Step "Handshake"

Revenue is the "ka-ching" moment. But in modern accounting (ASC 606 / IFRS 15), you can't just ring the bell whenever cash hits the bank. You have to earn the right to ring it.

Think of Revenue Recognition not as a calculation, but as a relationship timeline between you and the customer. We call this the Five-Step Model.

Step 1: The Agreement (Identify the Contract)

Before anything counts, there must be a "meeting of the minds." It doesn't need to be a 50-page document signed in blood. It can be a nod over a coffee counter.

The Litmus Test: If I deliver this, will you pay me? If the answer is "maybe" (because the customer is broke), you don't have a contract for accounting purposes yet.

Key Concept: No Commercial Substance = No Contract.

Step 2: The Promise (Identify Performance Obligations)

What are you actually doing for them? Are you selling a car, or are you selling a car plus a maintenance plan plus a GPS subscription?

The "Distinct" Rule: Can the customer use the item on its own?

Scenario: A construction firm builds a hospital. They buy bricks, glass, and steel. They aren't selling the client a pile of bricks; they are selling a hospital. The bricks are inputs, not distinct promises. That's one obligation.

Scenario: A software firm sells you a program and a separate training workshop. You could use the software without the workshop. These are two distinct obligations.

Step 3: The Price Tag (Determine Transaction Price)

This seems easy—look at the sticker, right? Not always.

Variable Consideration: What if there's a bonus for finishing early? Or a penalty for being late? You have to guess (estimate) the final price using the Expected Value (probability math) or the Most Likely Amount.

The "Time Travel" Tax: If a customer pays you today for work you'll do in 3 years, that money creates interest. You have to account for the Significant Financing Component.

Step 4: Splitting the Bill (Allocate the Price)

If you sold a bundle (Step 2), how much of the discount applies to the phone vs. the data plan?

The Fair Share: You can't just dump all the revenue into the bucket that makes you look best. You must allocate the total price based on the Standalone Selling Price (SSP).

The Logic: If the phone is usually $800 and the plan is usually $400, but you sold the bundle for $1,000, you have to split that $1,000 proportionally (2/3 to the phone, 1/3 to the plan).

Step 5: The Handover (Recognize Revenue)

This is the finish line. Revenue happens when Control transfers.

Point in Time: You buy a shirt. You walk out. You control the shirt. The store books the revenue now.

Over Time: You hire a painter for your house. You "control" the painted wall as he paints it. He doesn't wait until the very last brushstroke to book all the revenue; he books it gradually as the work gets done.

E. Income Measurement: The Art of Matching

If Revenue is the hero of the story, Expenses are the necessary sacrifices. Income Measurement is about ensuring the hero and the sacrifice appear in the same chapter.

1. The Matching Principle (The Golden Rule)

This is the heartbeat of accrual accounting. You must match the effort (expense) to the reward (revenue).

The Factory Example: You build a tractor in 2025. You pay for steel and labor in 2025. But you don't sell the tractor until 2026.

The Rule: The cost sits patiently in Inventory (an asset) until the sale happens. In 2026, when revenue is recorded, the cost moves to COGS. They "hit the books" holding hands.

2. Gains vs. Revenues (Core vs. Side-Hustle)

Revenue: Doing what you were born to do. (Starbucks selling coffee).

Gain: Getting lucky on a side deal. (Starbucks selling an old espresso machine for more than it's worth).

Why it matters: Investors pay for consistent Revenue; they are skeptical of one-time Gains.

3. Comprehensive Income (The "Hidden" Emotions)

Net Income is the headline, but it misses some deep currents. Other Comprehensive Income (OCI) captures value changes that haven't been "realized" yet.

Think of it like this: You own a house. Zillow says it went up in value by $50k. You feel richer (Equity up), but you haven't sold it yet, so you have no cash profit (Net Income unchanged). That's the essence of OCI.

The Formula: Net Income + OCI = Comprehensive Income.

F. The Atlantic Divide: U.S. GAAP vs. IFRS

The world is converging, but we aren't there yet. For the CMA, you need to know who allows what. Think of U.S. GAAP as the "Strict Rule-Follower" and IFRS as the "Principled Philosopher."

1. The Inventory Battle: LIFO vs. FIFO

U.S. GAAP: Loves LIFO (Last-In, First-Out). Why? Because when prices rise, LIFO lowers your profit (on paper), which lowers your taxes.

IFRS: Hates LIFO. Strictly prohibited. They argue that physically, no business sells their newest stuff first while letting the old stuff rot. It doesn't make sense physically, so they don't allow it financially.

2. The "Oops, I Was Wrong" Rule (Impairment Reversals)

You wrote down the value of a factory because the market crashed. Two years later, the market is booming. Can you write the value back up?

U.S. GAAP: No. Once it's written down, it stays down. We don't want managers manipulating profits by "un-impairing" assets.

IFRS: Yes. If the economy changes, the financial statements should reflect the new reality. You can reverse the loss (up to the original cost).

3. R&D: The Gambler vs. The Builder

You spend $1 million developing a new drug. Is that an Expense (money gone) or an Asset (investment)?

U.S. GAAP: It's an Expense. R&D is too risky; we don't know if it will work. (Exception: Software, once it's technically feasible).

IFRS: Splits it. Research is an expense (risky). Development can be capitalized (an asset) if you can prove the product will likely succeed.

Cheat Sheet: The "Rule of Thumb"

Feature	U.S. GAAP (The Strict Parent)	IFRS (The Flexible Parent)
Inventory	LIFO is okay (Tax reasons).	LIFO is banned (Illogical).
Impairment	No take-backs. Loss is permanent.	You can reverse the loss if value returns.
R&D	Expense it all (mostly).	Expense Research; Capitalize Development.
Fixed Assets	Historical Cost only.	Can use Revaluation (Market Value).

Planning, Budgeting, and Forecasting (20% - Levels A, B, and C)

Strategic planning

The 2026 Navigator: A CMA's Manifesto for Strategy in the Age of Chaos

The year is 2026. The leather-bound "Five-Year Strategic Plan" gathering dust on the CEO's shelf isn't just obsolete; it's a liability.

In today's hyper-volatile landscape, where AI algorithms shift market pricing in milliseconds and supply chains can snap due to a climate event halfway across the globe, strategy is no longer a document. It is a living, breathing nervous system.

For the Certified Management Accountant (CMA), this is the moment of metamorphosis. We are shedding the skin of the "scorekeeper." We are stepping into the cockpit as strategic navigators. The math is still our foundation, but the story behind the numbers is our product.

Here is how the future-ready CMA builds a strategy that survives contact with reality.
Phase 1: Reading the Radar (The Scan)

Before we decide where to sail, we must look at the weather and inspect the hull. In the old days, we called this "Environmental Scanning." Today, it's Survival Intelligence.

The Storm Outside (PESTLE 2.0) We don't just list factors anymore; we model collisions.

The Tech Tsunami: It's not just "is AI good?" It's asking, "Is a DeFi (Decentralized Finance) protocol about to eat our banking division?" or "Are deepfakes threatening our brand reputation?"

The Green Mandate: Environmental analysis isn't PR fluff. It's risk assessment. If our factory is in a zone where water is running out, our P&L is irrelevant. We are uninsurable.

The Social Shift: We watch Gen Alpha. They don't just buy products; they buy ethics. If we aren't carbon-neutral, we don't exist to them.

The Sharks in the Water (Porter's Five Forces) Competition in 2026 isn't fair.

New Entrants: The threat isn't another big corporation; it's two developers in a garage with an API that automates what we charge $500 an hour for.

The Power of Suppliers: When rare earth minerals for batteries are scarce, the supplier is king. We need to know who holds the cards.

** The Engine Room (Looking Inward)** We use SWOT and VRIO, but we strip away the ego.

VRIO is the Acid Test: We might think our proprietary software is a competitive advantage. But is it Rare? Is it Hard to Imitate? If a competitor can subscribe to a SaaS tool that does the same thing for $50/month, our "advantage" is a delusion.

Phase 2: The North Star (Purpose & Pulse)

In 2026, a company without a soul is a company without a future. Strategy requires a destination that encompasses more than just "Maximize Shareholder Wealth."

The "Why" Matters Vision statements used to be posters in the breakroom. Now, they are the glue holding remote teams together.

Mission: What are we building today?

Vision: What does the world look like if we succeed?

Values: What lines will we never cross, even if it costs us money?

Goals with Teeth (SMART & ESG) We still use SMART goals (Specific, Measurable, Achievable, Relevant, Time-bound), but the scorecard has changed. We operate on the Triple Bottom Line:

Profit: Because we need fuel.

People: Because burnt-out employees don't innovate.

Planet: Because there is no business on a dead rock.

The 2026 CMA ensures that an executive's bonus is tied as tightly to carbon reduction as it is to EBITDA.
Phase 3: The Nervous System (Alignment)

The greatest tragedy in business is the "Air Sandwich"—a disconnect between the visionary strategy at the top and the daily grind at the bottom.

Closing the Gap We need Cascading Goals (Hoshin Kanri). It's a game of catchball. The CEO says, "Take the hill." Middle management asks, "Do we have the ammo?" The frontline says, "The hill is muddy." They talk until the plan is realistic.

The Dashboard (Balanced Scorecard) Imagine driving a car looking only at the odometer (Financials). You'll run out of gas (Internal Process) or blow a tire (Learning & Growth) long before you reach the destination. The Balanced Scorecard forces us to look at the leading indicators:

Are our people learning fast enough?

Are our internal processes glitch-free?

Are our customers smiling?

Then... are we making money?

Phase 4: The War Room (Tactics & Models)

How do we win? We open the playbook.

The Garden (BCG Matrix) We have to be ruthless gardeners.

Stars: Feed them.

Cash Cows: Milk them to fund the Stars.

Dogs: The hardest part. In 2026, nostalgia is expensive. If a product is a "Dog," we kill it fast to save resources for the next big thing.

The Blue Ocean Why fight in shark-infested waters (Red Oceans) over penny margins? The goal is to innovate where no one else is looking. Don't build a better taxi; build Uber. Don't build a better circus; build Cirque du Soleil.

Multiverse Thinking (Scenario Planning) This is the CMA's superpower. We don't predict the future; we predict futures.

Scenario A: Tech boom, regulation light.

Scenario B: Global recession, supply chain collapse.

Scenario C: Strict carbon taxes introduced overnight. We build a strategy robust enough to survive all three.

Phase 5:

A strategy is only as good as the culture executing it.

Data > Ego The era of the "HiPPO" (Highest Paid Person's Opinion) is over. In 2026, the CMA brings the receipts. We replace "I feel like..." with "The predictive model shows..."

Agility is King The 5-year plan is now a 5-year vision with 90-day sprints. We must be willing to pivot. If the data changes on Tuesday, we change the plan on Wednesday.

Inclusivity The best strategic insights often come from the customer support rep, not the boardroom table. Successful strategy listens to the front lines.

A. The Bridge: Operations and Performance Goals

Think of a company's strategy as a destination on a map (e.g., "We want to be the #1 sustainable clothing brand"). The budget is the vehicle, the fuel, and the turn-by-turn navigation required to get there.

1. The Operational Budget: The "Living" Roadmap

In the old days, a budget was a static document locked in a drawer. In 2026, the operational budget is a living organism. It connects the "Cloud" (High-level Strategy) to the "Street" (Daily Operations).

Driver-Based Budgeting (The Logic): We no longer just guess dollar amounts. We look at the physical drivers of cost. If you run a delivery service, you don't just budget "$50,000 for gas." You build a formula:
Fuel_Budget=(Deliveries×Miles_Per_Delivery)÷MPG×Fuel_Pri ce

If your operations team optimizes routes and cuts miles by 10%, the budget automatically updates. This links physics to finance.

2. Performance Goals: The "Why"

A budget without a goal is just a list of expenses. To keep the budget human-centric, we use the Balanced Scorecard. This ensures we aren't burning out employees or angering customers just to save a dollar.

Financial: "Are we making money?" (e.g., Increase Net Margin).

Customer: "Do they like us?" (e.g., Reduce complaint resolution time).

Internal Process: "Are we efficient?" (e.g., Cut waste by 15%).

Learning & Growth: "Are we evolving?" (e.g., Upskill staff on AI tools).

3. Cascading: The Waterfall Effect

"Cascading" is the art of translation. You must translate the CEO's vision into the Janitor's daily goals.

CEO says: "Maximize Eco-Friendly Reputation."

Factory Manager hears: "Switch to biodegradable packaging."

Line Worker hears: "Keep material waste under 2%."

Result: Alignment. Everyone pulls the rope in the same direction.

B. The Process: Psychology Over Spreadsheets

A budget is 10% math and 90% psychology. The "Process" is how you get people to agree on the future.

1. The North Star (Strategic Alignment)

A budget must follow strategy, not history.

The Trap: Taking last year's budget and adding 2%. The Fix: If the strategy shifts from selling hardware to selling subscriptions, the budget must be torn down and rebuilt to fund software engineers, not factory parts.

2. The "IKEA Effect" (Participative Budgeting)

Psychology tells us that people value things more when they help build them. This is Participative Budgeting.

Top-Down: The Boss dictates the number. (Result: Resentment, unrealistic goals).

Bottom-Up: The Front-line Manager proposes the number. (Result: Ownership, better local knowledge).

The 2026 Standard: A hybrid conversation where the front line provides the reality check, and management provides the strategic boundary.

3. Rolling Forecasts: Driving with High Beams

The "Annual Budget" is like driving a car while looking only at the rear-view mirror. Rolling Forecasts mean you are always looking 12 months ahead. As January ends, you forecast next January. You never fall off the "fiscal cliff" at year-end.

C. Resource Allocation: The "Gardening" of Business

Economics is the study of scarcity. You have infinite dreams but limited cash. Resource allocation is the act of gardening: you must water the flowers (high potential projects) and pull the weeds (legacy costs).

1. The Trade-Offs

Every decision has an Opportunity Cost. If you spend $1M on a Super Bowl ad, that is $1M you cannot spend on R&D. The CMA requires you to master the art of choosing the path with the highest return.

2. Modern Allocation Methods

How do we decide who gets the water?

Method	The Analogy	Best For...
Incremental Budgeting	"Same as last year, plus a little."	Stable, boring departments (e.g., Rent, Utilities).
Zero-Based Budgeting (ZBB)	"Empty the closet and only put back what fits."	Shaking up "fat" organizations; eliminating legacy waste.
Activity-Based Budgeting (ABB)	"You get money based on the work you actually do."	Service departments; linking cost to volume.

The 2026 Shift: We are seeing a move toward Strategic Resource Allocation. This involves boldly cutting funds from profitable-but-slow "Cash Cows" to fund risky-but-fast "Stars."

D. The Toolbox: Mechanics and Tech

To navigate the 2026 landscape, you need to understand the machinery under the hood.

1. The Master Budget

This is the "Grand Unification" of all plans. It is a puzzle where every piece relies on the others.

- It starts with the Sales Budget (The Prediction).
- It ends with the Cash Budget (The Reality Check).
- If the Sales plan is wrong, the entire Master Budget fails.

2. Static vs. Flexible (The "Fairness" Factor)

Imagine a manager is given a budget to make 1,000 widgets. Suddenly, demand spikes, and she has to make 2,000. Her costs double.

Static Budget: Screams that she is "Over Budget" (Unfair).

Flexible Budget: Recalculates based on 2,000 units and says she did a great job (Fair).

Key Takeaway: Never judge performance against a static budget if volume has changed.

3. The Future is Now: AI & Analytics

The 2026 syllabus embraces the "Silicon Colleague."

Predictive Analytics: Using weather, social sentiment, and macro-economics to predict sales (replacing the "gut feeling").

Agentic AI: Software "agents" that watch the budget 24/7. They don't just report errors; they suggest fixes. "Alert: Shipping costs in Asia are up 15%. Recommend switching to Carrier B."

4. The Ethics of "Sandbagging"

Finally, the human element involves integrity. Budgetary Slack (Sandbagging) is when a manager intentionally lowers their revenue target to make it easy to hit so they get a bonus.

Why it's bad: It hides the company's true potential and ties up resources that could be used elsewhere.

The Fix: accurate data and a culture that rewards ambition, not just "hitting the number."

The 2026 CMA's Crystal Ball: A Survivor's Guide to Forecasting

Let's be honest: By the time 2026 rolls around, "Forecasting" won't look like a guy in a visor tapping away at a calculator. The CMA exam of the future acknowledges a hard truth: AI can crunch the numbers faster than you.

But AI is terrible at context. It can tell you that sales dropped, but it can't tell you it's because a competitor launched a viral TikTok campaign.

That is where you come in. The 2026 CMA isn't a calculator; they are a Data Translator. Your job isn't just to produce the number; it's to tell the story behind it.

Here is your human-centric guide to the "Big Three" forecasting tools: Regression, Learning Curves, and Expected Value.

I. Regression Analysis: The "BS Detector"

Think of Regression Analysis not as math, but as relationship counseling for data. You are trying to figure out if two things are actually dating, or if they just bumped into each other in the hallway.

In business terms: Does spending more on machine maintenance actually lower our defect rate?

The DNA of the Line

At its core, regression tries to draw a line through a cloud of messy dots. The equation is your map:

$Y=a+bX$

Y (The Destination): What you are trying to predict (Total Cost).

a (The Cover Charge): The Fixed Cost. The price of admission just to open the factory doors, even if you make nothing.

b (The Friction): The Variable Cost. How much pain (cost) do you add for every step (unit) you take?

X (The Gas Pedal): The Driver (Machine hours, miles driven, etc.).

The "So What?" Factor (R-Squared)

Here is where the 2026 CMA candidate shines. You can calculate the slope, but can you judge the reliability?

Enter R2 (The Coefficient of Determination). Think of R2 as a trust score between 0% and 100%.

R2=0.95: "These two are soulmates. Where X goes, Y follows." (Highly reliable for budgeting).

R2=0.20: "They are strangers." (Do not base a multi-million dollar budget on this).

The 2026 Reality Check: In the real world, beware of Multicollinearity. This is when your independent variables are copying each other (like using "labor hours" and "minutes worked" in the same model). It confuses the algorithm. Keep your variables independent!

II. Learning Curve Analysis: The "Gamer's Grind"

Have you ever played a difficult video game? The first time you fight the boss, it takes you 20 minutes and you panic. The second time? 15 minutes. By the tenth time, you're doing it in 5 minutes while drinking coffee.

That is the Learning Curve.

Corporations are just groups of humans. As they repeat tasks, they build muscle memory and find shortcuts. If you budget the 100th airplane to cost the same as the 1st, you will overprice your bid and lose the contract.

The Two Flavors (Don't Mix These Up!)

The CMA exam loves to trick you with the two different ways to measure this "leveling up."

Model	The Vibe	How it Works
Cumulative Average-Time (Wright)	The Group Project	As production doubles, the average time of ALL units drops. This assumes the entire batch gets faster.
Incremental Unit-Time (Crawford)	The Solo Sprinter	As production doubles, only that specific new unit gets faster. This curve is shallower and more conservative.

The Math of Experience

When the doubling isn't perfect (like predicting the 37th unit), we use the log model:

$Y=aXb$

Where b is your "learning index."

$b=\ln(2)\ln(\text{Learning Rate})$

The "Robot" Trap: In 2026, be careful applying this to fully automated factories. Robots don't "learn" unless you upgrade their software. If you apply an 80% human learning curve to a CNC machine, you are going to have a massive budget variance.

III. Expected Value: Poker for Accountants

The world is chaotic. Supply chains break. Pandemics happen. Trends die. Expected Value (EV) is how we turn "anxiety" into "algebra." It helps us play the odds.

The Logic

You are sitting at a table.

- Option A: A guaranteed $100 bill.
- Option B: A coin flip. Heads you get $250, Tails you get $0.

A "Risk Neutral" calculator says:
$EV=(0.50\times250)+(0.50\times0)=\$125$

Since $125 > $100, the math says flip the coin.

The "Perfect Info" Paradox

Sometimes, you can pay a consultant (or a super-advanced AI) to tell you the future. But how much is that info worth?

Value of Perfect Information (VOPI) = (Earnings with the crystal ball) - (Earnings without it).

The Golden Rule: If the consultant costs more than the VOPI, ghost them. You are better off taking the risk yourself.

The Human Element: Risk Appetite

Here is the nuance the 2026 exam demands. The math might say "Flip the coin" (EV $125 vs $100). But if getting $0 means the company goes bankrupt, the CMA must advise taking the guaranteed $100. Math calculates the average; Humans assess the survival.

The Verdict

Forecasting in 2026 isn't about memorizing the formula for Least Squares Regression (Excel does that). It's about:

Auditing the inputs: Is the data clean?

Selecting the tool: Do we need a Learning Curve (new manual product) or Regression (utility costs)?

Translating the output: Can you look the CFO in the eye and explain why the budget is lower next quarter?

The 2026 CMA: Taming the Financial Nervous System

In the dusty days of accounting past, a budget was a cage. It was a tool used by the "Department of No" to restrict movement and cap ambition.

But as we look toward the 2026 Certified Management Accountant (CMA) landscape, that definition is dead. In the modern era, a budget isn't a cage—it's a nervous system. It's the electric current that connects a CEO's vision on the top floor to the factory shift manager on the ground floor.

If you are stepping into the role of a CMA, you aren't just a number cruncher; you are an architect of value. You need to know that a Silicon Valley unicorn bleeds money differently than a Rust Belt manufacturer. One size fits nobody.

Here is your field guide to the six methodologies that define the financial pulse of a modern organization.

1. The Master Budget: The "Grand Chain" of Command

AKA: The Ecosystem

Think of the Master Budget not as a document, but as a row of dominoes. If the first one (Sales) wobbles, the last one (Cash) falls over.

This is the static roadmap for the year. It's the anchor. But its real beauty lies in its interdependence. In 2026, we don't operate in silos.

The First Domino: It all starts with the Sales Budget. If your sales team is hallucinating about selling 10,000 electric

SUVs, and the market only wants 5,000, the rest of your budget is fiction.

The Chain Reaction: Once Sales picks a number, Production calculates the metal needed. Procurement buys the tires. HR hires the hands to hold the wrenches.

The Reality Check: Finally, the Cash Budget tells you if you can afford to pay for all of this before the customers pay you.

The Human Reality: The Master Budget prevents the "Left Hand vs. Right Hand" disaster. It stops Marketing from launching a Super Bowl ad for a product that Production won't finish building until next July. It forces conversation.
2. Project Budgeting: The "Special Ops" Mission

AKA: The Life-Cycle View

The Master Budget runs on a calendar; Project Budgeting runs on a mission timeline. Whether it's building a new HQ or launching a vaccine, this budget has a birth and a death.

This is where the CMA becomes a futurist. You aren't just looking at today's bills; you are battling the Time Value of Money (NPV and IRR). You have to ring-fence cash for three years down the road, ensuring a project doesn't starve to death halfway through because of a bad quarter elsewhere.

The "Kill Switch": The most vital part of Project Budgeting in 2026 is the Milestone. We don't hand over $10 million on Day 1. We hand over $1 million to design the bridge. If the design fails? We freeze the remaining $9 million. This prevents the "Sunk Cost Fallacy"—the emotional trap of throwing good money after bad just because "we've already come this far."

3. Activity-Based Budgeting (ABB): The Efficiency Engine

AKA: The Reverse Engineer

Traditional budgeting is lazy. It looks at last year's spending and says, "Eh, let's just add 5% for inflation." That creates bloat.

ABB flips the script. It starts with the goal and works backward.

The Question: "We want to handle 100,000 customer calls. What does that physically require?"

The Math: 100,000 calls × 10 minutes per call = 1 million minutes. We need exactly X amount of staff at Y cost.

The Strategic Edge: ABB is the ultimate lie detector. If a department asks for $50,000 for "report generation," ABB forces the uncomfortable question: "Who actually reads those reports?" If the answer is "nobody," the activity—and the cost—gets cut. It connects dollars directly to muscle movement.

4. Zero-Based Budgeting (ZBB): The Marie Kondo Approach

AKA: The Clean Slate

ZBB is the most aggressive tool in the kit. It operates on a ruthless philosophy: You are entitled to nothing.

Every fiscal year, the budget resets to $0. It doesn't matter if you had $2 million last year. You have to justify every single dollar all over again as if the company were being born today.

The Survival Kit (Base Package): What is the bare minimum cash needed to keep the lights on?

The Wish List (Incremental Packages): You want new laptops? Prove the ROI. You want a team retreat? Justify the morale boost in dollars.

The Vibe Check: ZBB is incredible for killing "zombie costs"—those subscriptions nobody uses and legacy processes that don't make sense anymore. But be warned: it is exhausting. It requires high energy. Smart companies don't do this every year for everyone; they rotate it through departments to avoid burnout.

5. Continuous (Rolling) Budgets: The Headlights

AKA: Agility Over Accuracy

Static budgets have a fatal flaw: they go stale. A budget written in December is often useless by June because the world has changed.

Imagine driving a car at night. A static budget is a map you memorized before you left the house. A Rolling Budget is your headlights—they move with you, always illuminating the next 12 months.

How it works: As January 2026 ends, you don't just mark it "done." You immediately add January 2027 to the end of your plan. You are always looking one full year ahead.

Why it matters: This eliminates the "Fiscal Cliff"—that frantic week in December where managers waste money buying useless office chairs just to "use up the budget" so they don't lose it next year. Rolling budgets keep the team focused on the horizon, not the calendar year-end.

6. Flexible Budgeting: The Truth Serum

AKA: Apples-to-Apples

This is the fairest way to judge a human being's performance.

Imagine Sarah, a factory manager. She budgeted $100k to make 10,000 units. At the end of the year, she spent $120k.

The Static View: "Sarah is $20k over budget! She failed!"

The Reality: Demand exploded, and Sarah actually produced 15,000 units.

The Flexible Budget Fix: We recalculate the budget based on what actually happened. If she made 15,000 units, she should have spent $150k. Since she only spent $120k, she didn't fail—she's a hero who saved the company $30k through efficiency.

The Takeaway: Static budgets judge the spend. Flexible budgets judge the performance. It separates "Sales Volume noise" from "Operational Efficiency signal."
The CMA's Toolkit

In 2026, you don't pick one of these and ignore the rest. You are a financial craftsman, and these are your tools.

Use the Master Budget to keep the banks happy.

Use ZBB when the company gets fat and complacent.

Use Rolling Budgets when the market is volatile and unpredictable.

Use Flexible Budgets so you don't fire your best managers by mistake.

Annual profit plan and supporting schedules

The Crystal Ball in the Boardroom: Master Budgeting for the 2026 Strategist

Let's be honest: for decades, the "Master Budget" had a reputation problem. It was viewed as the corporate equivalent of eating your vegetables—a dry, static spreadsheet cooked up in October, locked in a drawer in January, and completely irrelevant by March.

Welcome to 2026. That world is gone.

In today's volatile economy, the Annual Profit Plan isn't a spreadsheet; it's a simulation. It is the closest thing a Certified Management Accountant (CMA) has to a time machine. It allows you to travel twelve months into the future, make mistakes, run out of cash, and crash the company—all within the safety of a predictive model—so you can fix the course before real money is lost.

For the modern strategist, the budget is a living, breathing nervous system connecting the shop floor to the C-suite. Here is how we build this roadmap in the age of AI and real-time analytics.

Part A: The Operational Budget (The "Hustle")

This is the engine room. Before we talk about bank accounts or buying new factories, we have to figure out the actual work of the business.

1. The Sales Budget: The Prophecy

It all begins here. If this number is wrong, everything else is fiction. In the past, a sales manager would lick their finger, hold it to the wind, and say, "Let's do last year plus 5%."

In 2026, we don't guess. We use predictive intelligence. Imagine EcoMoto, our electric scooter startup. Their sales budget isn't a single number; it's a "Scenario Cloud." Their AI analyzes urban traffic patterns, competitor price drops, and even impending weather systems (people don't buy scooters in rainy Q1s).

The 2026 Shift: We rarely budget for a single outcome. We budget for the "Most Likely" scenario but stress-test for the "Worst Case."

Budgeted Sales=AI Forecasted Units×Dynamic Price per Unit

2. The Production & Inventory Dance

Once we know what the market wants, we have to decide what to build. This is a high-stakes balancing act known as the Goldilocks Dilemma:

Too little inventory? You suffer stockouts and angry customers.

Too much inventory? You have cash tied up in batteries and tires gathering dust.

We calculate the precise number of units to build to keep the shelves full but the warehouse lean:

Units to Produce=Sales Demand+Safety Stock Target−What We Already Have

3. The Ingredients: Materials, Labor, and Overhead

Now, the budget gets granular.

Direct Materials (DM): The procurement team engages here. It's not just about buying aluminum; it's about when we pay for it.

Direct Labor (DL): This line item is evolving fast. As factories automate, the "Labor" line shrinks, but the cost per hour skyrockets because you aren't paying for manual assembly—you're paying for highly skilled robotics technicians.

Manufacturing Overhead (MOH): The catch-all bucket. Rent, electricity, lubricants. The modern CMA splits this relentlessly into Variable (moves with the volume) and Fixed (stays flat even if we sell nothing).

Part B: The Financial Budget (The "Pulse")

You can have a brilliant product and record-breaking sales, but if you run out of cash on a Tuesday, you are bankrupt by Wednesday. The Financial Budget is the health check that ensures the organism survives.
1. The Cash Budget: The Survival Kit

This is the single most important document for the CFO. It is the heartbeat of the organization. In 2026, we don't do annual cash budgets; we do Rolling Cash Forecasts.

The Inflow: Just because you sold a scooter in January doesn't mean you have the money. If the customer pays in 60 days, you are "profit rich" but "cash poor."

The Outflow: Suppliers and employees need to be paid now.

The Gap: The Cash Budget predicts the terrifying gap between the two.

Why it matters: If EcoMoto sees a cash deficit projected for March, they can secure a line of credit today. If they wait until March, the bank will say no.

2. The Pro-Forma Financials

These are your "Ghost Statements." They look exactly like your real Income Statement and Balance Sheet, but they represent a future that hasn't happened yet. They allow management to look at the projected Year-End results and ask: "Are we happy with this picture? If not, what do we change today?"

Part C: The Capital Budget (The "Legacy")

While Operational Budgets are about surviving the year, Capital Budgets are about defining the decade. This is where we decide to build the new Gigafactory or acquire a competitor.

The Decision Matrix (2026 Edition)

We used to just look at NPV (Net Present Value)—essentially, "will this machine make more money than it costs?" While the math (NPV>0) is still king, the variables have changed.

Enter the ESG Factor. In 2026, a capital project isn't just evaluated on dollars. It's evaluated on Impact.

Option A: A coal-powered generator. High immediate ROI, but massive carbon tax liability and reputational damage.

Option B: Solar infrastructure. Lower immediate ROI, but tax credits and "Green Goodwill" with Gen Z consumers.

The modern Capital Budget integrates these "soft" metrics into hard numbers, proving that sustainability is often the superior financial choice.

The Butterfly Effect: A Warning for the CMA Candidate

If you are studying for the CMA exam, do not make the mistake of viewing these budgets as separate islands. They are a delicate ecosystem.

Consider the Chain Reaction:

Marketing decides to cut the ad budget to save money (SG&A Budget).

Sales forecasts drop by 10% (Sales Budget).

Production slows down, meaning we buy fewer batteries (DM Budget).

Because we buy fewer batteries, we lose our bulk discount from the supplier, raising the cost per unit.

Cash Collections dry up because sales dropped (Cash Budget).

The company no longer has the liquidity to pay for the new solar plant (Capital Budget).

The Takeaway: An authentic, high-value CMA doesn't just calculate the numbers; they interpret the story. They stand at the intersection of the past and future, translating strategy into the only language that everyone understands: Actionable Reality.

Top-level planning and analysis

The year is 2026. The era of the accountant as a mere "scorekeeper" is dead and buried.

Today, if you are a Certified Management Accountant (CMA), you are not just balancing ledgers; you are the Architect of Uncertainty. In a world run by autonomous finance and AI that can crunch a decade of variance analysis in seconds, your value isn't in calculation—it's in interpretation.

Top-Level Planning has evolved into the central nervous system of the modern corporation. It is the bridge between the rigid "what happened" (Historical Data) and the probable "what might happen" (Future Strategy).

This guide reimagines the three pillars of strategic planning—Pro Forma Income, Financial Projections, and Cash Flow—not as academic exercises, but as survival tools for the modern financial leader.
Part A: Pro Forma Income – The Art of Truth-Telling

In 2026, GAAP (Generally Accepted Accounting Principles) is still the law, but it is rarely the whole truth. GAAP is rigid; business is messy.

Pro Forma (Latin for "as a matter of form") is your mechanism to cut through the static. It is the story of your company's economic reality stripped of the one-time chaos that confuses investors.

The Signal vs. The Noise

Imagine looking at a heart monitor. A sudden sneeze causes a massive spike on the graph. Is the patient dying?

No, they just sneezed. Pro Forma is the act of removing the "sneeze" so you can read the heartbeat.

In the algorithmic age, we look for two types of noise to filter out:

The "Digital Pivot" Costs: In 2026, almost every company is undergoing massive restructuring to integrate robotics or AI. Closing an old factory to open a fully automated one incurs massive severance costs. These are real costs, but they don't reflect the future profitability of the automated plant. Pro Forma adds them back.

The "Paper" Losses: Goodwill impairment or asset write-downs. These make the net income look terrible, but no cash actually left the bank account.

The Ethical Razor's Edge

Here lies the danger. Pro Forma is powerful, but it is also the tool of choice for charlatans. This is the "Dark Arts" of finance—stripping out "bad stuff" like marketing costs or R&D just to make the bottom line look pretty.

The 2026 Guardrails: You must adhere to the SEC's Regulation G. Think of this as your ethical compass:

No Hiding: You cannot bury the GAAP loss in a footnote while shouting the Pro Forma profit from the rooftops. They must stand side-by-side.

The Bridge: You must provide a clear reconciliation—a map showing exactly how you got from the messy GAAP number to the clean Pro Forma number.

Part B: Financial Projections – Building the Digital Twin

You can no longer forecast an Income Statement in a vacuum. If you pull a thread on Revenue, the Balance Sheet moves, and the Cash Flow vibrates.

In 2026, we don't just "forecast"; we build a Digital Twin of the corporation.

The "Growing Broke" Paradox

The most counter-intuitive concept in finance is that success can kill you.

Imagine a company that grows sales by 50% overnight. It sounds like a dream, but it's a logistical nightmare. To sell 50% more, you need 50% more inventory and 50% more accounts receivable (customers who haven't paid you yet).

If you don't have the cash to fund that inventory before the customers pay you, you are insolvent. You are profitable on paper, but bankrupt in reality.

The Calculus of Survival: EFN

To prevent "growing broke," we calculate External Funds Needed (EFN). This formula answers the question: "How much cash do we need to raise to afford this growth?"

$$EFN=(S0A*)\Delta S-(S0L*)\Delta S-(M\times S1\times RR)$$

The Human Translation:

Usage of Funds $(S0A*)\Delta S$: "We need to buy more assets to support the new sales."

Spontaneous Funding $(S0L*)\Delta S$: "Our vendors will float us some of that cost (Accounts Payable)."

Internal Funding ($M \times S1 \times RR$): "We can pay for some of it using our own profits."

If the result is positive, you have a Funding Gap. You need to call the bank. Today.

Part C: Cash Flow – Oxygen vs. Nutrition

Here is the immutable law of business physics: Profit is nutrition. Cash is oxygen. You can go weeks without food (profit). You cannot go five minutes without oxygen (cash).

The AI Advantage in 2026

In the old days, we assumed customers paid in "30 days" because the contract said so. Today, AI tools analyze behavioral data. The AI knows that Client X says Net 30, but historically pays on Day 42.

Short Term (Direct Method): The "Checkbook" view. Who are we paying this Friday? When does the payroll hit? This is about keeping the lights on.

Long Term (Indirect Method): The "Strategic" view. This starts with Net Income and works backward to see if the business model generates cash or consumes it.

The Holy Grail: Free Cash Flow (FCF)

$FCF = \text{Operating Cash Flow} - \text{Capital Expenditures}$

This is the only metric that truly matters to investors. It asks: After keeping the factory running and the lights on, is there any cash actually left over to grow?

Case Study: The CyberDyne Dilemma

The Situation: You are the Lead CMA for CyberDyne Robotics. It is late 2025. The CEO wants to aggressively expand sales by 25% in 2026.

The Data:

Current Sales (S0): 10,000,000

Assets: The factory is at full capacity. Every new robot sold requires new machinery. The Capital Intensity is 60% (0.60).

Liabilities: Vendors finance about 20% (0.20) of growth.

Profit: You run a tight ship with a 10% Net Margin.

Dividends: The shareholders demand their cut. You retain 60% of profits (Retention Ratio).

The Question: Can CyberDyne afford this growth on its own?

The Calculation:

The Growth: Sales are jumping by $2,500,000.

The Cost (Asset Increase): To sell that much, you need new assets.
0.60×$2,500,000=$1,500,000 needed.

The Help (Liabilities): Vendors will float you part of the bill.
0.20×$2,500,000=$500,000 covered.

The Reinvestment (Retained Earnings): You will earn profit on these new sales.
New Sales ($12.5M)×10% Margin×60% Retention=$750,000 earned.

The Verdict (EFN):
EFN=$1,500,000 (Need)−$500,000 (Vendor Help)−$750,000 (Internal Profit)
EFN=$250,000

The Strategy: Despite being profitable, CyberDyne will run out of cash. You are short $250,000. Your job as the CMA is not just to report this number, but to solve it. You must advise the CFO to secure a line of credit or issue stock before the year begins. If you wait until the cash runs out, it's too late.

Performance Management (20% - Levels A, B, and C)

Cost and variance measures

Cost and Variance Measures: A 2026 Perspective for the Certified Management Accountant

The landscape of management accounting has shifted dramatically. By 2026, the Certified Management Accountant (CMA) is no longer just a keeper of historical ledgers but a strategic partner navigating a volatile, data-rich global economy. The era of static spreadsheets has given way to dynamic, AI-driven insights where cost management is inextricably linked with data analytics, supply chain resilience, and Environmental, Social, and Governance (ESG) metrics.

This comprehensive guide explores the core pillars of cost and variance measures, reimagined for the 2026 professional standard.

A. Comparison of Actual to Planned Results

The Evolution of the Feedback Loop

At its heart, the comparison of actual results to planned expectations is the primary feedback mechanism for any organization. It is the "reality check" that tells management whether they are winning or losing. In the traditional sense, this was a retrospective exercise—looking at last month's numbers to see where money leaked.

However, in the 2026 business environment, this comparison has become near-instantaneous. We are moving away from the "post-mortem" approach toward "real-time diagnostics." Modern Enterprise Resource

Planning (ERP) systems now ingest data continuously, allowing for a comparison of actuals to plans not just monthly, but daily or even hourly.

The Strategic Necessity of Variance

Why do we compare? It is not merely to assign blame. The comparison serves three critical functions:

Strategic Alignment: It ensures that the capital deployed is actually moving the company toward its long-term goals. If the plan was to enter a new market and the actuals show zero marketing spend in that region, the strategy is disconnected from execution.

Operational Control: It acts as the guardrail for daily operations. If actual energy costs spike 15% above plan on a Tuesday, an automated alert allows a floor manager to investigate a malfunctioning machine immediately, rather than waiting for a month-end report.

Organizational Learning: It highlights the quality of the planning process itself. Persistent deviations often suggest that the plan was unrealistic, not that the execution was flawed.

Static vs. Dynamic Comparisons

A major pitfall in this area is the "Static Budget" trap. Comparing actual results directly to a static master budget is often like comparing apples to oranges, especially if sales volume has changed.

Example: Imagine a manufacturer of biodegradable packaging planned to produce 10,000 units with a budget of $100,000. Due to a sudden surge in demand (perhaps a new regulation banning plastic), they actually produce 15,000 units and spend $140,000.

If we simply compare Actual ($140,000) to Static Plan ($100,000), it looks like they overspent by $40,000. This is misleading. They actually produced more units efficiently. This necessity for context leads us directly to the use of flexible budgets.

B. Use of Flexible Budgets to Analyze Performance
The Concept of "Flexing"

A flexible budget is a budget that adjusts or "flexes" for changes in the volume of activity. It is the gold standard for performance evaluation because it strips away the noise created by volume fluctuations. In 2026, flexible budgeting is often automated within algorithmic planning software, which instantly recalculates expected costs based on the actual output achieved.
The Two-Step Analysis

To truly understand performance, a CMA breaks down the total variance into two distinct components:

Sales Volume Variance: This measures the difference between the Static Budget and the Flexible Budget. It answers the question: "How much profit did we gain or lose simply because we sold more or less than we thought we would?" This is the responsibility of the sales and marketing teams.

Flexible Budget Variance: This measures the difference between the Flexible Budget and Actual Results. It answers the question: "Given that we produced X units, did we spend more or less than we should have?" This is the responsibility of the production and cost center managers.

Why This Matters in a Volatile Economy

In an era defined by supply chain disruptions and rapid shifts in consumer preference, volume is rarely stable.

If a factory manager is judged against a static budget during a downturn (low volume), they might look like a hero because their total spending is low, even if they are wasting materials per unit.

Conversely, during a boom, they might be penalized for "overspending" total dollars, even if they are operating at peak efficiency per unit.

2026 Application: Consider a cloud computing firm. Their "direct material" is server energy usage. If client demand doubles (volume), their energy bill should double. A flexible budget accounts for this. If the energy bill triples while demand only doubles, the flexible budget variance exposes an efficiency problem (perhaps cooling systems are failing), separating it from the revenue growth.

C. Management by Exception

The Signal and the Noise

In a data-rich world, managers are drowning in information. "Management by Exception" is the disciplined practice of focusing attention only on those areas where results deviate significantly from the plan. It is about filtering out the noise to hear the signal.

Setting the Thresholds

To make this work, an organization must define what constitutes a "significant" deviation. This is often based on:

Absolute Dollar Amount: "Investigate any variance over $5,000."

Percentage: "Investigate any variance exceeding 5% of the standard."

Statistical Control: Using standard deviations (sigma) to trigger alerts only when a process is statistically out of control.

The Shift to Predictive Exception Management

Traditionally, management by exception was reactive—you waited for the variance to happen. In the 2026 landscape, aided by predictive AI, we see a shift to Pre-emptive Management by Exception.

Machine learning models now analyze trends to flag "exceptions in the making."

Example: A dashboard might alert a CMA: "Current labor efficiency has dropped 2% every hour for the last four hours. At this rate, we will hit a reportable unfavorable variance by 4:00 PM."

This allows the manager to intervene before the financial damage is crystallized. This moves the CMA from a "scorekeeper" to a "performance driver."

Management by exception also respects human cognitive limits. It prevents decision fatigue. By trusting the system to handle the routine (the 95% of transactions that go as planned), leaders can dedicate their creative energy to solving the complex problems (the 5% exceptions)—such as a supply chain bottleneck or a sudden change in tariff regulations.

D. Use of Standard Cost Systems

The Blueprint of Efficiency

A standard cost system records transactions using "standard" (predetermined) costs rather than actual costs. It is, effectively, a blueprint of what costs should be under efficient operating conditions.

Components of Standard Cost

For a manufactured product, the standard cost per unit is built from three pillars:

- Direct Materials: Standard Quantity × Standard Price.
  - Example: 2 kg of Lithium at $15/kg.
- Direct Labor: Standard Hours × Standard Rate.
  - Example: 3 hours of assembly at $25/hour.
- Manufacturing Overhead:
  - Variable Overhead: Applied based on an activity driver (e.g., machine hours).
  - Fixed Overhead: A lump sum allocated across expected production volume.

Standard Costing in 2026: The ESG Integration

A major evolution in the 2026 CMA syllabus is the integration of sustainability into standard costing. Companies are now setting standards not just for financial costs, but for Carbon Costs and resource intensity.

Carbon Standards: A product might have a "Standard Carbon Footprint" of 50kg CO_2e.

Water Usage Standards: A standard of 100 liters per unit.

Variances are now reported on these non-financial metrics alongside the dollars. If a department uses cheaper materials (Favorable Price Variance) but those materials require more energy to process (Unfavorable Carbon Variance), the standard cost system captures this trade-off, preventing "greenwashing" or short-sighted cost cutting.

Ideal vs. Practical Standards

Ideal Standards: Assume perfection (no waste, no breaks). These are motivating but rarely achieved.

Practical (Attainable) Standards: Allow for normal waste and downtime. These are used for financial planning and cash flow forecasting because they are realistic.

2026 Trend: Dynamic Standards. Rather than setting a standard once a year, AI adjusts standards quarterly based on rolling averages of global commodity prices, keeping the benchmark relevant.

E. Analysis of Variation from Standard Cost Expectations

This is the forensic accounting aspect of the job. When actuals deviate from standards, we decompose the difference into specific "buckets" to find the root cause.

1. Direct Material Variances

Price Variance: (Actual Price−Standard Price)×Actual Quantity Purchased.

Cause: Did the purchasing manager negotiate poorly? Did global lithium prices spike? Did we switch to a higher-quality supplier?

Usage (Quantity) Variance: (Actual Quantity Used−Standard Quantity Allowed)×Standard Price.

Cause: Did the machines malfunction and ruin material? Are the workers untrained?

2. Direct Labor Variances

Rate Variance: (Actual Rate−Standard Rate)×Actual Hours.

Cause: Did we use senior technicians for a junior job? Did overtime trigger a 1.5x pay rate?

Efficiency Variance: (Actual Hours−Standard Hours Allowed)×Standard Rate.

Cause: Is morale low? Was there a power outage? This is often the most controllable variance for floor managers.

3. Overhead Variances

These are more complex and include:

Spending Variance: Did we spend more on electricity/supplies than budgeted for the actual hours worked?

Efficiency Variance: Did we run the machines longer than necessary (driving up variable costs) to produce the output?

Volume Variance: Did we produce fewer units than the denominator level used to calculate the fixed overhead rate? (This is a capacity utilization metric).

Investigation Triggers

In 2026, variance analysis is cross-functional. An unfavorable material usage variance might not be the factory's fault—it could be the purchasing department buying substandard cheap material (favorable price variance) that breaks easily (unfavorable usage variance). The CMA's job is to connect these dots.
Hypothetical Financial Transaction & Problem Solving Scenario: Apex Batteries Ltd. (2026)

Apex Batteries manufactures specialized solid-state battery packs for electric motorcycles. The company uses a standard cost system. For the month of October 2026, the company planned to produce 1,000 units but actually produced 1,200 units due to a rush order.

Standard Cost Card (Per Unit):

Direct Materials (Lithium-X): 4 kg at $20.00 per kg.

Direct Labor: 2 hours at $30.00 per hour.

Actual Results for October 2026:

Production: 1,200 units.

Materials Purchased and Used: 5,000 kg at a total cost of $95,000.

Direct Labor: 2,300 hours at a total cost of $71,300.

Problem: As the CMA for Apex, calculate the following variances and explain the "story" behind the numbers to the Board of Directors:

Direct Material Price Variance

Direct Material Usage Variance

Direct Labor Rate Variance

Direct Labor Efficiency Variance

Solution and Explanation
1. Direct Material Variances

A. Material Price Variance

Formula: $(AP-SP)\times AQ$

Calculation:

Actual Price (AP) = $95,000/5,000 kg=$19.00 per kg.

Standard Price (SP) = $20.00 per kg.

Actual Quantity (AQ) = 5,000 kg.

Variance = ($19.00−$20.00)×5,000=−$1.00×5,000=$5,000 Favorable.

B. Material Usage Variance

Formula: (AQ−SQ)×SP

Calculation:

Actual Quantity (AQ) = 5,000 kg.

Standard Quantity Allowed (SQ) = 1,200 units×4 kg/unit=4,800 kg.

Variance = (5,000−4,800)×$20.00=200 kg×$20.00=$4,000 Unfavorable.

2. Direct Labor Variances

A. Labor Rate Variance

Formula: (AR−SR)×AH

Calculation:

Actual Rate (AR) = $71,300/2,300 hours=$31.00 per hour.

Standard Rate (SR) = $30.00 per hour.

Actual Hours (AH) = 2,300 hours.

Variance = ($31.00−$30.00)×2,300=$1.00×2,300=$2,300 Unfavorable.

B. Labor Efficiency Variance

Formula: (AH−SH)×SR

Calculation:

Actual Hours (AH) = 2,300 hours.

Standard Hours Allowed (SH) = 1,200 units×2 hours/unit=2,400 hours.

Variance = (2,300−2,400)×$30.00=−100 hours×$30.00=$3,000 Favorable.

Board of Directors Analysis (The Story)

"Members of the Board, here is the operational analysis for October:

We successfully met the increased demand of 1,200 units. Financially, our Material Price Variance was $5,000 Favorable. We secured Lithium-X at $19 instead of $20. However, this appears to have come at a quality cost. The Material Usage Variance was $4,000 Unfavorable, indicating we used 200kg more material than standard. It is highly probable that the cheaper material was of lower grade, leading to higher scrap rates during production.

On the labor side, we see a Rate Variance of $2,300 Unfavorable. This suggests we either paid overtime to meet the rush order or used more senior staff. However, this investment paid off. The Efficiency Variance was $3,000 Favorable. Our team worked faster than standard (taking 2,300 hours instead of the expected 2,400).

Conclusion: The net variance is minimal, but the trade-off is clear. We saved money on purchasing but lost some of it on waste. We paid more for labor per hour but got higher productivity in return. For November, I recommend reviewing the quality of the $19 Lithium supplier to ensure the waste doesn't increase further."

Responsibility Centers and Reporting Segments: A Comprehensive Analysis for the 2026 CMA

In the modern landscape of corporate governance and strategic financial management, the ability to decentralize operations while maintaining control is paramount. As organizations grow, the centralized "command and control" model becomes obsolete, replaced by a structure of delegated authority known as decentralization. This shift necessitates a robust framework for performance evaluation, ensuring that managers across the organization make decisions that align with the company's overall goals—a concept known as goal congruence.

The following analysis provides a full account of responsibility centers, transfer pricing, contribution margins, and segment reporting. It is tailored to the evolving standards of the Certified Management Accountant (CMA) curriculum for 2026, integrating traditional cost accounting principles with modern emphases on strategic analytics, data-driven decision-making, and updated regulatory frameworks like FASB ASC 280.

2a. Types of Responsibility Centers

A responsibility center is any organizational unit, department, or division where a specific manager is held accountable for the unit's activities and performance. The core philosophy here is "controllability": managers should only be evaluated based on the items they can significantly influence.

In the 2026 business environment, we categorize these centers into four distinct types, each with increasing levels of authority and autonomy.

1. Cost Centers

A Cost Center is a segment where the manager has control over costs but not over revenue or the use of investment funds. The primary objective is to minimize costs while maintaining a specified level of quality and service.

Metric for Evaluation: Performance is typically measured using variance analysis—comparing actual costs against standard or flexible budget costs.

Examples:

Manufacturing Department: The painting department of an automobile factory. The manager controls labor hours and paint usage but does not sell the cars.

IT Support Desk: A corporate helpdesk does not generate revenue; its goal is to resolve tickets efficiently within budget.

HR Department: Responsible for recruitment and training costs, but generates no direct profit.

Strategic Note: In modern "lean" organizations, cost centers are often pressured to become "profit centers" by charging internal users for services (e.g., IT charging departments for support).

2. Revenue Centers

A Revenue Center is a segment where the manager is responsible primarily for generating sales revenue. These managers have little control over the manufacturing cost of the product or the investment in assets, though they may control marketing and selling expenses.

Metric for Evaluation: Sales volume, total revenue, and price variances.

Examples:

Regional Sales Office: A software company's "North American Sales Team." Their goal is to hit booking targets.

Reservation Department: In an airline or hotel chain, the team taking bookings is judged on the revenue secured.

3. Profit Centers

A Profit Center manager is accountable for both revenues and costs, and therefore, the resulting profit. This is a significant step up in autonomy. The manager must balance the drive to increase revenue with the discipline to control costs.

Metric for Evaluation: Segment Margin, Gross Profit, or Operating Income.

Examples:

Retail Store: A specific location of a Walmart or Target. The store manager orders inventory (cost) and manages staff (cost) while driving sales (revenue).

Bank Branch: A local branch manager controls loan generation (revenue) and operating expenses like tellers and utilities.

4. Investment Centers

The Investment Center represents the highest level of decentralization. The manager is responsible for revenues, costs, and the efficient use of the assets (capital) invested in the division. They have the authority to make major capital expenditure decisions, such as expanding a factory or entering a new market.

Metric for Evaluation: Return on Investment (ROI), Residual Income (RI), and increasingly, Economic Value Added (EVA).

Examples:

Regional Subsidiary: The "European Division" of Coca-Cola. The President of this division decides where to build bottling plants (investment) and manages the P&L.

Product Group: The "PlayStation Division" at Sony. They manage R&D investment, production costs, and sales revenue.

2b. Transfer Pricing

When one division of a company sells goods or services to another division within the same company, the price charged for this internal transaction is called the Transfer Price.

Transfer pricing is one of the most contentious areas in management accounting because it creates a natural conflict. The selling division wants a high price to maximize its own profit, while the buying division wants a low price to minimize its costs. Corporate headquarters, however, cares only about the total company profit.
Objectives of Transfer Pricing

Goal Congruence: The price should encourage division managers to make decisions that maximize total company profits, not just their own.

Performance Evaluation: The price should allow both the selling and buying divisions to be evaluated fairly.

Autonomy: It should preserve the autonomy of division managers, avoiding constant interference from headquarters.

Primary Transfer Pricing Methods

1. Market-Based Transfer Pricing (The Gold Standard) If a perfectly competitive external market exists for the product, the market price is the optimal transfer price.

Why? It represents the true opportunity cost. If the selling division transfers internally, it gives up a sale to an outside customer. Therefore, it should be compensated at the market rate.

Example: A crude oil division selling to the refining division. Since there is a global price for crude oil, that price is used.

2. Cost-Based Transfer Pricing Used when no external market exists, or the product is unique.

Variable Cost: Transferring at variable cost ensures the buying division buys internally (good for the company), but the selling division makes zero profit (bad for morale/evaluation).

Full Cost (Absorption Cost): Includes fixed overhead. This is dangerous because it passes the selling division's inefficiencies to the buyer.

Cost-Plus: Full cost plus a markup (e.g., 10%). This guarantees a profit for the seller but may result in a price higher than the market, leading the buyer to shop outside (suboptimal).

3. Negotiated Transfer Pricing The buying and selling managers sit down and bargain.

Range of Negotiation:

Floor (Minimum Price): The selling division's variable cost + any opportunity cost (lost contribution margin from outside sales).

Ceiling (Maximum Price): The market price the buying division would pay an outside supplier.

Pros/Cons: It respects autonomy but can be time-consuming and often depends more on the managers' negotiating skills than economic reality.

CMA 2026 Update - The "Dual Pricing" Approach: In complex modern firms, companies sometimes use Dual Pricing. The selling division is credited with the market price (to encourage production), while the buying division is charged the variable cost (to encourage internal purchasing). The difference is eliminated in a consolidation account at headquarters.

2c. Contribution Margin

The Contribution Margin (CM) is a fundamental concept in Cost-Volume-Profit (CVP) analysis and is critical for short-term decision-making.

Contribution Margin=Sales Revenue−Total Variable Costs

Understanding the Logic

The CM represents the portion of sales revenue that is not consumed by variable costs and is therefore available to "contribute" to covering fixed costs. Once fixed costs are covered, any remaining CM is pure profit.

Key Components:

Variable Costs: Costs that change in direct proportion to volume (e.g., direct materials, direct labor, variable shipping).

Fixed Costs: Costs that remain constant regardless of volume (e.g., rent, insurance, salaries).

Strategic Applications

Break-Even Analysis: knowing the CM per unit allows managers to calculate exactly how many units must be sold to cover all costs.

Special Order Decisions: If a customer places a one-time bulk order at a discounted price, the manager should accept it if the price exceeds the variable cost (positive contribution margin), assuming ample capacity exists.

Product Mix Decisions: When resources are limited (e.g., limited machine hours), companies should prioritize products with the highest Contribution Margin per unit of the constrained resource, not necessarily the highest profit per unit.

2d. Reporting of Organizational Segments

Reporting financial information by segment is vital for stakeholders to understand the risks and returns of a diversified company. For the 2026 CMA, this involves understanding both Internal Reporting (Managerial Accounting) and External Reporting (Financial Accounting / GAAP).

Internal Reporting: The Contribution Approach

For internal decision-making, traditional absorption costing income statements (which mix fixed and variable costs) are misleading. Instead, management accountants use the Contribution Margin Income Statement.

The Format:

Sales

(-) Variable Costs

(=) Contribution Margin

(-) Traceable Fixed Costs: Costs that exist only because the segment exists (e.g., salary of the segment manager, maintenance on segment machines). If the segment disappears, these costs disappear.

(=) Segment Margin: This is the most important metric for evaluating the long-term profitability of a segment.

(-) Common Fixed Costs: Costs that support the entire company (e.g., CEO salary, HQ rent). These should never be allocated to segments for performance evaluation because segment managers cannot control them.

(=) Net Operating Income

Crucial Distinction: The Contribution Margin tells us how the segment performs in the short run (volume changes). The Segment Margin tells us if the segment is viable in the long run (covering its own specific bills).

External Reporting: FASB ASC 280 (The "Management Approach")

For external financial statements (10-K), US GAAP (FASB ASC 280) requires public companies to report segment information.

The Management Approach: Companies must define segments externally exactly the same way the Chief Operating Decision Maker (CODM) views them internally. If the CEO reviews data by geographic region, the external reports must be by geographic region.

Quantitative Thresholds: A segment must be reported separately if it meets 10% of the combined revenue, profit, or assets of all operating segments.

2025/2026 Updates (ASU 2023-07): Recent updates now require more granular disclosure of significant segment expenses. Companies must disclose significant segment expenses that are regularly provided to the CODM. This increases transparency, preventing companies from hiding inefficiencies within broad "aggregated" cost lines.

Hypothetical Financial Transaction & Problem Solving

Scenario: TechNovation Inc. has two divisions:

Chip Division: Manufactures advanced silicon processors.

Phone Division: Assembles smartphones.

The Phone Division currently buys a specific processor (Model X1) from an outside supplier for $160 per unit. The Chip Division produces a similar processor (Model X1-Internal) which it sells to outside customers for $175.

Chip Division Data:

Variable Cost per unit: $90

Full Capacity: 50,000 units

Current External Sales: 40,000 units

Phone Division Requirements: 15,000 units

The Conflict: The Phone Division wants to buy 15,000 units from the Chip Division. The Chip Division manager refuses to sell for less than $175 (market price). The Phone Division manager argues, "It only costs you $90 to make! Charge me $110, and we both win."

Problem:

Calculate the minimum transfer price the Chip Division should accept.

Calculate the maximum transfer price the Phone Division should pay.

Determine if the transfer should take place from the perspective of the company as a whole.

Solution & Explanation:

Step 1: Analyze Capacity The Chip Division has a capacity of 50,000 units and sells 40,000 externally.

Idle Capacity: 10,000 units.

Units needed by Phone Division: 15,000 units.

Conflict: To fulfill the order, the Chip Division can use the 10,000 idle units, but must displace (give up) 5,000 units of external sales.

Step 2: Calculate Minimum Transfer Price (Seller's Floor) The minimum price must cover the variable cost plus any lost contribution margin (opportunity cost) on displaced sales.

For the first 10,000 units (Idle Capacity):

Opportunity cost is $0 (no lost sales).

Minimum Price = Variable Cost = $90.

For the remaining 5,000 units (Displaced Sales):

The Chip Division loses the sale to an outside customer at $175.

Contribution Margin lost = Market Price ($175) - Variable Cost ($90) = $85.

Minimum Price = Variable Cost ($90) + Opportunity Cost ($85) = $175.

Weighted Average Minimum Price: 15,000(10,000×$90)+(5,000×$175)=15,000900,000+875,000 =15,0001,775,000=$118.33

The Chip Division manager must receive at least $118.33 per unit to be as well off as they are currently.

Step 3: Calculate Maximum Transfer Price (Buyer's Ceiling) The Phone Division will not pay more than it costs to buy from the outside supplier.

Outside Supplier Price = $160.

Step 4: Conclusion

Minimum (Floor): $118.33

Maximum (Ceiling): $160.00

Since the Maximum ($160) is greater than the Minimum ($118.33), there is a bargaining range. The transfer should take place.

Financial Impact: If the transfer occurs (e.g., at $140), the company saves money.

Cost to Make (Internal): $118.33 (Average cost including opportunity cost)

Cost to Buy (External): $160.00

Savings per unit: $41.67

Total Corporate Savings: $41.67 \times 15{,}000 = \$625{,}050$.

Final Recommendation: TechNovation HQ should mandate the transfer or encourage negotiation, as producing internally saves the company over $600k compared to buying from the outside supplier.

2026 CMA Relevance Summary

For the 2026 CMA exam, candidates must move beyond simple calculation. You must demonstrate the ability to:

Analyze Ethics: Is it ethical for the Chip manager to inflate costs during negotiation?

Performance Measures: The 2026 Strategic Framework

In the evolving landscape of 2026, performance measurement has shifted from simple historical accounting to predictive, data-driven strategic alignment. The modern management accountant does not just report what happened; they analyze why it happened and what will happen next. The following sections detail the critical performance measures required for the Part 1 CMA exam, enhanced with modern analytics and behavioral economics.

a. Product Profitability Analysis

In the past, companies often relied on broad averages to determine if a product was making money. Today, with the rise of Activity-Based Costing (ABC) and AI-driven cost attribution, we can see the granular truth. Product profitability analysis is the process of linking revenues generated by a specific product to the expenses incurred to design, make, market, and deliver it.

The "Peanut Butter" Problem Traditional costing spreads overheads like "peanut butter"—evenly across all products. This is dangerous. It makes complex, low-volume products appear profitable when they are actually draining resources.

Modern Application: In 2026, we use Life-Cycle Costing. We don't just look at manufacturing costs; we look at the "cradle-to-grave" costs. This includes R&D, marketing, and crucially, the disposal or recycling costs required by new ESG (Environmental, Social, and Governance) regulations.

Example: Consider a tech firm selling two tablets: the "Pro" (high volume, simple) and the "Elite" (low volume, custom parts).

Traditional View: Both have the same 40% margin because overhead is allocated by labor hours.

ABC View: The "Elite" requires 80% of the engineering team's time for updates and special handling in shipping. Its true margin is likely negative (-10%). The "Pro" is subsidized by the "Elite."

Action: The firm should either re-price the "Elite" to reflect its true consumption of resources or discontinue it.

b. Business Unit Profitability Analysis

When a company grows, it often splits into decentralized units (divisions, subsidiaries). The challenge is ensuring these units act in the company's best interest. Business unit profitability measures the economic value added by a specific segment.

Controllable vs. Uncontrollable Costs A key principle in the CMA curriculum is the Controllability Principle. You should only evaluate a manager on costs they can influence.

Controllable Margin: Revenue minus Variable Costs minus Traceable Fixed Costs. This is the best measure of the manager's performance.

Segment Margin: Controllable Margin minus Common Fixed Costs (allocated corporate overhead). This measures the business unit's viability, not the manager's skill.

Transfer Pricing Friction Profitability often depends on "Transfer Prices"—the price one division charges another for goods. If the Battery Division charges the Car Division too much for batteries, the Car Division looks unprofitable, even if the company as a whole is making money.

c. Customer Profitability Analysis

Not all revenue is good revenue. This is the most critical shift in modern analytics. Some customers demand so much service, support, and customization that they actually destroy value.

The Whale Curve We use a visual tool called the "Whale Curve" to demonstrate this.

The Top 20%: These customers typically generate 150% to 200% of the company's total profit. They are low-maintenance and high-volume.

The Middle: These customers break even.

The Bottom 20%: These customers lose the company money (bringing the total profit back down to 100%).

Example: A logistics company has a client, "BigRetail," that demands 24/7 support, frequent expedited shipping, and small batch orders. While BigRetail pays $1 million in revenue, the Cost to Serve (expediting fees, overtime labor) is $1.1 million. The company is losing $100,000 annually on its "biggest" client. The solution isn't always firing the customer; it might be implementing a "menu of services" where expedited shipping costs extra, shifting BigRetail back into profitability.

d. Return on Investment (ROI)

ROI is the grandfather of performance metrics. It is popular because it is a percentage, making it easy to compare a small division to a giant one.

The Formula:
ROI=Average Investment CapitalOperating Income

DuPont Analysis (The "Why" of ROI): To fix a low ROI, you need to know what broke. DuPont analysis splits ROI into two levers:

Profit Margin (Are we keeping enough of every dollar earned?)

Asset Turnover (Are we using our machines and inventory efficiently?)

ROI=(SalesNet Income)×(Total AssetsSales)

The Danger of ROI: Underinvestment ROI has a fatal flaw. It discourages managers from investing in new, profitable projects if those projects have a lower return than the division's current ROI. This is called "sub-optimization." A manager running a division with a 25% ROI might reject a project offering a 20% return, even if the company's cost of capital is only 10%. They reject it to keep their average high, hurting the company in the long run.
e. Residual Income (RI)

To solve the behavioral issues of ROI, we use Residual Income. RI is not a percentage; it is a dollar amount. It measures the absolute wealth created over and above the required return.

The Formula:
Residual Income=Operating Income−(Required Rate of Return×Investment)

Why It Is Better: RI aligns the manager's goals with the company's goals (Goal Congruence). If a project has a return higher than the company's required rate (e.g., 10%), the RI will be positive. The manager will accept the project because it increases the total dollar value of their bonus pool, even if it slightly lowers their average percentage return.

f. Investment Base Issues

Both ROI and RI rely on defining the "Investment" (the denominator). How we value assets changes the result dramatically.

Gross Book Value (Historical Cost): This ignores depreciation. It keeps the investment base steady.

Net Book Value (Depreciated Cost): This is the most common method but causes the "Aging Asset Artifice." As assets get older, their book value drops (due to depreciation). If income stays the same, ROI artificially skyrockets.

Result: Managers are incentivized to keep old, inefficient machinery rather than upgrading, just to keep their ROI looking high.

Fair Value: Using the current market value of assets. This is the most accurate economic measure but is subjective and hard to track.

g. Key Performance Indicators (KPIs)

KPIs are the navigational instruments of the business. In 2026, the focus is on a mix of Leading and Lagging indicators.

Lagging Indicators (The Rearview Mirror): These tell you what happened. Examples: Net Income, ROI, Customer Churn Rate. They are accurate but too late to change.

Leading Indicators (The Windshield): These predict the future. Examples: Employee Satisfaction Scores (predicts productivity), Number of New Patents (predicts future revenue), Website Traffic (predicts sales).

The SMART Rule: KPIs must be Specific, Measurable, Achievable, Relevant, and Time-bound. A vague goal like "improve quality" is not a KPI. "Reduce defect rate to <1% by Q3" is a KPI.

h. Balanced Scorecard

Developed by Kaplan and Norton, the Balanced Scorecard prevents "tunnel vision" where managers focus only on short-term financials. It forces a view of the business from four perspectives. In 2026, this concept has evolved to heavily integrate Sustainability.

Financial Perspective: "How do we look to shareholders?" (ROI, Cash Flow).

Customer Perspective: "How do customers see us?" (Satisfaction, Market Share).

Internal Process Perspective: "What must we excel at?" (Cycle time, Quality control).

Learning and Growth Perspective: "Can we continue to improve?" (Employee training, IT infrastructure).

The Strategy Map: This connects the dots. "If we train our employees (Learning), they will fix the machines faster (Internal Process), which reduces delivery times for clients (Customer), leading to higher sales (Financial)."

Hypothetical Financial Transaction & Problem Solving

Scenario: You are the Divisional Manager of the "GreenTech" division at Solaris Corp.

Current Operating Assets: $5,000,000

Current Operating Income: $900,000

Company's Required Rate of Return (Cost of Capital): 12%

The Opportunity: A new project is available. It requires an investment of $1,000,000 in new machinery. This machinery will generate $140,000 in additional annual operating income.

The Problem:

Calculate the current ROI.

Calculate the ROI with the new project. Will you accept the project if your bonus is based on ROI?

Calculate the current Residual Income (RI).

Calculate the RI with the new project. Will you accept the project if your bonus is based on RI?

Solution and Explanation

1. Current ROI Calculation:
ROI=5,000,000900,000=18%

2. ROI with New Project:

New Total Income = $900,000 + $140,000 = $1,040,000

New Total Assets = $5,000,000 + $1,000,000 = $6,000,000
NewROI=6,000,0001,040,000=17.3%

Decision (ROI Basis): REJECT. Even though the project makes money, it drags your average performance down from 18% to 17.3%. If you are judged on ROI, you will say no to a profitable venture.

3. Current Residual Income (RI):
RI=Income−(Assets×12%)
RI=900,000−(5,000,000×0.12)
RI=900,000−600,000=$300,000

4. RI with New Project:

First, let's see the RI of just the project:
Project
RI=140,000−(1,000,000×0.12)=140,000−120,000=+$20,000

New Total RI:
Total RI=1,040,000−(6,000,000×0.12)
Total RI=1,040,000−720,000=$320,000

Decision (RI Basis): ACCEPT. The project adds $20,000 of pure economic value to the company. Your total Residual Income rises from $300,000 to $320,000.

Conclusion on the Transaction: This example perfectly illustrates why Residual Income is often superior for Goal Congruence. It encourages managers to take on any project that exceeds the cost of capital, whereas ROI incentivizes managers to protect their percentage, often at the expense of company growth.

Cost Management (15% - Levels A, B, and C)

Measurement concepts

1. Types of Cost and Cost Behavior

Understanding cost behavior is the "physics" of management accounting. Just as a physicist must know how gravity acts on an object, a management accountant must know how costs react to changes in activity levels. In 2026, we don't just guess these behaviors; we use data analytics to pinpoint them.

A. The Core Behaviors

Variable Costs: These are the costs that dance in perfect sync with your production volume. If you produce zero units, your variable cost is zero. If you double production, your total variable cost doubles, yet the cost per unit remains constant.

Example: Think of the lithium-ion batteries in an electric vehicle (EV). If you make one car, you need one battery pack. If you make 1,000 cars, you need 1,000 packs. The cost per battery doesn't change, but the total bill sure does.

Fixed Costs: These are the stubborn costs. They do not care how much you produce (within a relevant range). They are total costs that remain constant regardless of activity, meaning the cost per unit drops as production rises.

Example: The rent on the EV factory. Whether you assemble one car or 10,000 cars this month, the landlord expects the same rent check.

Mixed (Semivariable) Costs: These are the hybrids. They have a baseline fixed component (to have the service ready) and a variable component (based on usage).

Example: An industrial electricity bill. You pay a connection fee (fixed) plus a charge for every kilowatt-hour used to run the robots (variable).

Step Costs: These costs stay flat for a while and then jump abruptly once a threshold is crossed.

Example: Quality Control Supervisors. One supervisor can oversee 20 workers. If you hire the 21st worker, you must hire a second supervisor. The cost "steps" up instantly.

B. The Relevant Range This is a critical concept for the 2026 exam. Cost behavior assumptions (linear variable costs, flat fixed costs) are only valid within a specific "band" of activity, called the relevant range. Outside this range, chaos ensues—rent might go up if you need a bigger building, or supplier discounts might kick in for massive bulk orders.

2. Actual and Normal Costs

This distinction explains when and how we assign overhead to products. It is the difference between "waiting for the bill" and "estimating the bill."

A. Actual Costing In an Actual Costing system, you assign the exact costs incurred to the product.

Direct Materials (DM): Actual price × Actual quantity.

Direct Labor (DL): Actual rate × Actual hours.

Overhead (OH): Actual overhead incurred.

The Problem: You often don't know your actual utility or repair bills until the end of the month (or year). This delays product costing and creates fluctuating unit costs due to seasonal variances (e.g., heating costs in winter).

B. Normal Costing This is the industry standard for timeliness. We "normalize" the volatility of overhead.

DM & DL: Still tracked at Actual cost.

Overhead: Applied using a Predetermined Overhead Rate (POHR).

Formula: Total Estimated Overhead Costs ÷ Total Estimated Allocation Base (e.g., machine hours).

The Benefit: You can cost a job the moment it is finished.

The Catch: At year-end, you will have "Over-applied" or "Under-applied" overhead because your estimate was inevitably slightly wrong. You must then adjust Cost of Goods Sold (COGS) to fix the variance.

3. Standard Costs

Standard costing is the "budgeted benchmark." It answers the question: What should this product cost if we work efficiently?

A. The Components of a Standard A standard is not an average; it is a target. It consists of two parts for every input:

Price Standard: How much should we pay per unit of input? (e.g., $10 per kg of steel).

Quantity Standard: How much input should we use per unit of output? (e.g., 5 kg of steel per widget).

B. Variance Analysis (The "Why") When actual results differ from standards, we get variances.

Favorable (F): Actual cost < Standard cost.

Unfavorable (U): Actual cost > Standard cost.

We break these down into Price Variances (did we pay too much?) and Usage/Efficiency Variances (did we waste material or time?).

Example: If your factory used cheap, low-quality plastic (Favorable Price Variance) but the machines kept jamming and wasting material (Unfavorable Usage Variance), standard costing helps you pinpoint that the "cheap" purchase was actually a mistake.

4. Absorption (Full) Costing

Absorption costing is the "Rule Follower." It is the only method acceptable for external financial reporting (GAAP/IFRS) in 2026.

The Philosophy: Every product you make acts like a sponge (absorbent). It must soak up all manufacturing costs—both variable and fixed—necessary to create it.

The Formula: Product Cost = Direct Materials + Direct Labor + Variable Manufacturing Overhead + Fixed Manufacturing Overhead.

The Impact on Income: Because Fixed Overhead (FOH) is attached to the inventory, if you produce more than you sell, some FOH stays "trapped" in the warehouse on the Balance Sheet. This defers the expense to a future period, artificially inflating Net Income in the current period. This creates a dangerous incentive for managers to overproduce just to boost bonuses.

5. Variable (Direct) Costing

Variable costing is the "Internal Decision Maker." It is not allowed for external tax or GAAP reporting, but it is vital for internal strategy.

The Philosophy: Fixed costs (like factory rent) are "Period Costs." They happen because time passed, not because we made a specific unit. Therefore, they should be expensed immediately, not attached to the product.

The Formula: Product Cost = Direct Materials + Direct Labor + Variable Manufacturing Overhead. (Note: Fixed Manufacturing Overhead is treated as a lump-sum expense on the Income Statement below the Contribution Margin line).

The Strategic Advantage: Variable costing reveals the Contribution Margin (Sales minus Variable Costs). This is critical for Break-Even Analysis and "Special Order" pricing decisions. It removes the incentive to overproduce because producing unsold inventory does not hide fixed costs.

6. Joint and By-Product Costing

In many industries (oil refining, dairy, lumber), one raw material naturally breaks into multiple products.

A. The Process

Joint Costs: The costs incurred before the products split apart (e.g., the cost of raising a cow).

Split-off Point: The moment the raw material separates into distinct products (e.g., milk and cream).

Separable Costs: Costs incurred after the split-off to finish the products.

B. Allocation Methods Since joint costs cannot be traced directly to a specific product, we must allocate them arbitrarily:

Physical Measure: Allocate based on weight or volume (e.g., gallons). Simple, but ignores value (allocating heavy costs to low-value scrap).

Sales Value at Split-off: Allocates more cost to the product that generates more revenue immediately.

Net Realizable Value (NRV): Used if products need further processing. Allocates based on final sales value minus separable processing costs.

C. By-Products These are incidental outputs with low value (e.g., sawdust from a lumber mill). We generally do not allocate joint costs to them. Instead, any revenue from selling by-products is typically treated as a reduction in the cost of the main products or as "Other Income."
Hypothetical Financial Transaction & Problem

The Scenario: The "SolarGlide" Hoverboard Company: Zenith Mobility Inc. (Uses Standard Costing & Absorption Costing). Product: Produces high-end hoverboards.

Situation: In October 2026, Zenith processes a specialized raw material "Graphite-X."

Data for October 2026:

Production: Zenith processed 10,000 kg of Graphite-X (Joint Cost: $200,000).

At the split-off point, this yielded two products:

Product A (Decks): 6,000 units. Sales value at split-off: $30/unit.

Product B (Wheels): 4,000 units. Sales value at split-off: $20/unit.

Manufacturing (Product A only):

Standard Direct Labor: 2 hours per unit at $25/hour.

Actual Direct Labor: 12,200 hours total, costing $292,800.

Sales: Sold 5,000 units of Product A. (1,000 units remain in inventory).

The Problem:

Allocate the $200,000 Joint Costs using the Sales Value at Split-off Method.

Calculate the Direct Labor Rate Variance and Direct Labor Efficiency Variance for Product A.

Determine the final value of Product A Ending Inventory assuming Absorption Costing (including the allocated joint cost and standard labor, ignoring overhead for simplicity in this step).

Solution and Explanation

Step 1: Allocate Joint Costs (Sales Value at Split-off)

First, calculate the total revenue potential at the split-off point.

Product A Revenue: 6,000 units × $30 = $180,000

Product B Revenue: 4,000 units × $20 = $80,000

Total Revenue: $180,000 + $80,000 = $260,000

Now, find the percentage share for each:

Product A Ratio: $180,000 / $260,000 ≈ 69.23%

Product B Ratio: $80,000 / $260,000 ≈ 30.77%

Allocate the $200,000 Joint Cost:

Allocated to Product A: $200,000 × 69.23% = $138,462 (rounded)

Cost per unit for A: $138,462 ÷ 6,000 units = $23.08 per unit (Joint Cost portion)

Step 2: Calculate Labor Variances (Standard Costing)

Standard Rate (SR): $25.00/hr

Actual Hours (AH): 12,200 hours

Actual Cost: $292,800

Actual Rate (AR): $292,800 ÷ 12,200 = $24.00/hr

Standard Hours Allowed (SH): 6,000 units produced × 2 hrs/unit = 12,000 hours

Calculation A: Labor Rate Variance Difference in pay rate × Actual hours worked. Formula: AH×(AR−SR) 12,200×($24.00−$25.00)=12,200×(−$1.00) = $12,200 Favorable (Explanation: We paid workers $1.00 less per hour than budgeted.)

Calculation B: Labor Efficiency Variance Difference in hours used × Standard pay rate. Formula: SR×(AH−SH) $25.00×(12,200−12,000)=$25.00×200 = $5,000 Unfavorable (Explanation: Workers worked 200 hours more than the standard allowed for 6,000 units.)

Step 3: Value Ending Inventory (Absorption Basis)

We have 1,000 units of Product A unsold. We need the cost per unit.

Joint Cost Component: $23.08 (calculated in Step 1)

Direct Labor Component (Standard): 2 hours × $25 = $50.00

Note: Under standard costing, we value inventory at Standard, not Actual. Variances are expensed to COGS.

Total Standard Cost per Unit: $23.08 + $50.00 = $73.08

Ending Inventory Value: 1,000 units × $73.08 = $73,080

2a. Job Order Costing: Precision in Customization

The Core Concept

Job Order Costing is the methodology of tracing costs to a specific "job," project, or contract. Unlike mass production where every unit is identical, Job Order Costing is used when products are distinct. Think of a law firm handling a specific divorce case, a construction company building a custom bridge, or a marketing agency designing a unique campaign for a client.

In 2026, the definition remains the same, but the application has changed. We no longer rely solely on manual time sheets. We now use Internet of Things (IoT) sensors and automated time-tracking software to assign direct costs with pin-point accuracy.

The Three Cost Components

To understand Job Order Costing, you must understand the "Holy Trinity" of manufacturing costs that flow into the Work-in-Process (WIP) inventory:

Direct Materials (DM): The raw stuff you can physically see in the product. In a custom furniture shop, this is the mahogany wood.

Direct Labor (DL): The hands-on time spent by workers. This is the carpenter sawing the wood.

Manufacturing Overhead (MOH): This is where it gets tricky. These are indirect costs—factory rent, electricity, glue, supervisor salaries—that cannot be traced to one specific table.

The Overhead Application Problem

Since we cannot trace the electric bill to a single table, we must allocate it. We use a Predetermined Overhead Rate (POHR).
POHR=Estimated Total Amount of the Allocation BaseEstimated Total Manufacturing Overhead Cost

Example: Imagine a custom drone manufacturer, "SkyHigh Bots." They estimate their annual overhead (rent, utilities) will be $1,000,000. They believe the main driver of these costs is Direct Labor Hours, estimated at 20,000 hours for the year.
POHR=20,000 hours$1,000,000=$50 per direct labor hour

If a specific job (Job #101) takes 10 hours of labor, we add $500 ($50 × 10) of overhead to that job's cost sheet.
2026 Update: The Digital Job Sheet

In the 2026 CMA environment, the "Job Cost Sheet" is digital and live.

Authentic Application: A specialized custom sneaker company uses RFID tags on shoe soles. As the sneaker moves from the "Stitching Station" to the "Painting Station," the system automatically logs the time.

Verifiable Benefit: This eliminates "human error" where employees guess how many hours they spent on a project at the end of the week. Real-time data means the "Actual Cost" is available instantly, allowing managers to pivot if a job is running over budget before it is finished.

Key Takeaway: Job Order Costing is about uniqueness. If you can distinguish one unit of output from another, you use this system.

2b. Activity-Based Costing (ABC): The Truth-Teller

The Core Concept

Traditional costing (like the Job Order example above) often gets it wrong because it uses "volume-based" drivers like labor hours to spread overhead. This is dangerous. It assumes that a complex product uses the same amount of overhead as a simple product, just because they took the same time to assemble.

Activity-Based Costing (ABC) is a microscope. It recognizes that activities cause costs, and products consume activities.

The Hierarchy of Costs

To implement ABC, you must break down costs into a hierarchy. This is a favorite topic for CMA essay questions.

Unit-Level Activities: Done for every single unit (e.g., drilling a hole in metal).

Batch-Level Activities: Done for a group of units (e.g., setting up a machine). You set up the machine once, whether you run 1 unit or 1,000 units.

Product-Sustaining Activities: Done to support a specific product line (e.g., designing a prototype).

Facility-Sustaining Activities: General costs that keep the lights on (e.g., factory security).

The Two-Stage Allocation Process

Stage 1: Assign resource costs to "Activity Cost Pools" (e.g., Machining Pool, Setup Pool, Quality Control Pool).

Stage 2: Allocate these pools to products using "Activity Drivers" (e.g., Machine hours, Number of setups, Number of inspections).

2026 Update: Time-Driven ABC (TDABC) and AI

The biggest criticism of ABC has always been that it is expensive and time-consuming to interview employees to ask, "How much time do you spend on setups?"

In 2026, we use Time-Driven ABC (TDABC) powered by AI.

Authentic Scenario: A hospital uses ABC to cost patient surgeries. Instead of asking nurses how long they spend charting, the hospital's ERP system logs the timestamp when a nurse enters a room and when they leave.

Algorithm: The AI calculates the "Cost per Minute" of the resource (the nurse) and automatically applies it to the patient (the cost object) based on the exact digital time log.

Strategic Value: This reveals "Unused Capacity." If you pay for 10,000 hours of nursing time but only assign 8,000 hours to patients, you have 2,000 hours of idle capacity. Traditional systems hide this; ABC exposes it.

Pros and Cons in the Modern Era

Pros Cons

Accurate Profitability: Reveals that some "high revenue" customers are actually losing money because they demand too much service (high "cost-to-serve").

Complexity: Requires maintaining two systems (one for GAAP/External reporting, one for internal management).

Better Pricing: Allows companies to price based on the actual resources consumed. Data Overload: With modern sensors, you can have too much data. Managers must filter noise to find signal.

2c. Life-Cycle Costing: The Cradle-to-Grave Perspective

The Core Concept

Most accounting systems focus on the production phase—the time when the factory is actually making the widget. Life-Cycle Costing (LCC) takes a step back. It tracks costs from the initial R&D spark, through design, production, marketing, distribution, customer service, and finally, disposal.

This is the most critical system for the 2026 CMA because of the integration of ESG (Environmental, Social, and Governance) standards.

The Three Stages of Life-Cycle Costing

Upstream Costs (R&D and Design): This is where 80% of a product's costs are "locked in." Once you design a car to use steel instead of aluminum, you have committed to the cost of steel for the product's life. LCC emphasizes spending more here to save money later.

Manufacturing Costs: The traditional production costs (DM, DL, MOH).

Downstream Costs (Marketing, Distribution, Disposal): The costs to sell, service, and eventually recycle the product.

2026 Update: The "Circular Economy" Mandate

In the past, "disposal" was an afterthought. In 2026, regulations (especially in the EU and California) require companies to take responsibility for their product's end-of-life.

Extended Producer Responsibility (EPR): A verifiable trend where electronics manufacturers must pay for the recycling of their old devices.

The "Shadow Price" of Carbon: Companies now factor in the cost of carbon emissions over the product's life. If a cheaper material creates more emissions during disposal, LCC will flag it as "expensive" because of potential carbon taxes or regulatory fines.

Example: A washing machine company can use cheap plastic gears (saving $10 in manufacturing). However, these gears break after 2 years, leading to high warranty claims and early disposal fees. LCC analysis would show that using metal gears (costing $15) is actually cheaper over the full life cycle because it reduces warranty costs and extends the product's life, improving brand sustainability ratings.

Strategic Insight: LCC is not just about cost control; it is about Target Costing. We determine the market price the customer will pay, subtract our desired profit margin, and the remainder is the "Target Cost" we must achieve across the entire life cycle.

2d. Other Costing Systems
1. Process Costing

Used for mass production of identical units (cement, oil, flour).

The Mechanism: Costs are accumulated by department, not by job.

Equivalent Units: The key calculation. If you have 1,000 buckets of paint that are 50% full at the end of the month, you technically have 500 "Equivalent Units" of paint. You must spread costs over these theoretical completed units.

2. Backflush Costing

A "Lean" accounting method used in Just-In-Time (JIT) environments.

The Logic: Traditional accounting tracks every movement: Raw Materials → WIP → Finished Goods. This is waste.

The Method: Backflush costing waits until the product is finished or even sold, and then "flushes" all costs backward to the accounts in one entry. It eliminates the detailed tracking of WIP.

Risk: You lose visibility of WIP. It only works if your cycle time is very fast (e.g., hours, not weeks).

3. Kaizen Costing

Japanese for "Continuous Improvement."

The Approach: Unlike standard costing, which sets a standard and tries to meet it, Kaizen costing assumes the standard should decrease every period.

2026 Context: Companies use AI to identify micro-efficiencies (e.g., reducing machine idle time by 4 seconds) to continually lower the cost base.

4. Throughput Accounting (Theory of Constraints)

Focuses on the speed at which the system generates money.

The Constraint: Every factory has a "bottleneck." Throughput accounting argues that you should only worry about costs at the bottleneck.

Throughput = Sales - Totally Variable Costs.

Goal: Maximize throughput while keeping operating expenses stable.

Hypothetical Financial Transaction & Problem Solving
The Scenario: "Eco-Tech Batteries Inc."

Background: Eco-Tech manufactures advanced batteries for electric vehicles. They currently use a traditional Job Order Costing system based on Direct Labor Hours. However, the CFO believes this is distorting costs because their new "Green-Cell" line requires complex robotic setups and specialized hazardous waste disposal (ESG factors), whereas the "Standard-Cell" line is simple and manual.

Data for the Month:

Overhead Budget: $2,000,000 total.

Driver: Direct Labor Hours (Total estimated: 50,000 hours).

Two Jobs Completed:

Job A (Standard-Cell): 1,000 units. Requires 200 Labor Hours. Direct Materials: $10,000. Direct Labor Cost: $4,000.

Job B (Green-Cell): 100 units. Requires 50 Labor Hours. Direct Materials: $20,000. Direct Labor Cost: $1,000.

The Shift to ABC (Activity-Based Costing): The CFO proposes an ABC system with two cost pools:

Robotic Setups: Pool Cost = $1,500,000. Driver = Number of Setups. (Total Setups = 150).

Waste Processing (ESG): Pool Cost = $500,000. Driver = Pounds of Hazardous Waste. (Total Waste = 10,000 lbs).

Activity Usage:

Job A: 1 Setup, 50 lbs of waste.

Job B: 5 Setups, 500 lbs of waste (complex, dirty process).

The Problem:

Calculate the total cost of Job B using the Traditional (Job Order) method.

Calculate the total cost of Job B using the Activity-Based Costing (ABC) method.

Explain the solution and the strategic implication for 2026.

The Solution
1. Traditional Method (Job Order Costing)

Step 1: Calculate Predetermined Overhead Rate (POHR).
POHR=50,000 hours$2,000,000=$40 per Direct Labor Hour

Step 2: Assign Costs to Job B.

Direct Materials: $20,000

Direct Labor: $1,000

Overhead: 50 Hours × $40/hour = $2,000

Total Cost (Traditional):
$20,000+$1,000+$2,000=$23,000

2. Activity-Based Costing (ABC) Method

Step 1: Calculate Activity Rates.

Robotic Setup Rate: 150 Setups$1,500,000=$10,000 per Setup

Waste Processing Rate: 10,000 lbs$500,000=$50 per lb

Step 2: Assign Overhead to Job B.

Setups: 5 Setups × $10,000 = $50,000

Waste: 500 lbs × $50 = $25,000

Total ABC Overhead = $50,000 + $25,000 = $75,000

Step 3: Calculate Total Cost.

Direct Materials: $20,000

Direct Labor: $1,000

Overhead (ABC): $75,000

Total Cost (ABC):
$20,000+$1,000+$75,000=$96,000

Explanation and Strategic Analysis

The Shocking Difference: Under the Traditional system, we thought Job B cost $23,000. Under ABC, we realize it actually costs $96,000.

Why did this happen? This is a classic case of Cross-Subsidization.

The Traditional system allocated overhead based on Labor Hours. Since Job B (robotic, high-tech) used very little human labor (only 50 hours), it attracted very little overhead cost ($2,000).

However, Job B is actually extremely expensive to support. It requires 5 complex robotic setups and generates massive amounts of hazardous waste. The Traditional system ignored these complexities.

Job A (the simple product) was likely being "over-costed" to subsidize the losses of Job B.

Strategic Implication for the 2026 CMA: If Eco-Tech had continued using the Traditional system, they might have priced Job B at $30,000, thinking they were making a profit. In reality, they were losing $66,000 on every batch!

Furthermore, the Waste Processing cost highlights the ESG factor. By identifying that waste costs $50 per lb, the company now has a financial incentive to redesign the Green-Cell battery to be cleaner (Life-Cycle Costing), fulfilling both profit and sustainability goals.

3a. Fixed and Variable Overhead Expenses

In 2026, the distinction between fixed and variable overhead has become more nuanced due to the shift toward Service-as-a-Software (SaaS) models and usage-based billing in industrial operations.
The Behavior of Costs

1. Fixed Overhead Fixed overhead costs remain constant in total, regardless of changes in activity levels (within a relevant range). However, on a per-unit basis, they decrease as production volume increases—a concept known as operating leverage.

Classical Examples: Factory rent, insurance, straight-line depreciation of machinery, and the salary of the plant manager.

2026 Context: In modern "Lights-Out" manufacturing (fully automated factories), fixed costs have exploded. The depreciation of robotics, amortization of AI software licenses, and cybersecurity infrastructure are now massive fixed overheads.

Example: A semiconductor plant incurs $5 million monthly in "clean room" maintenance and air filtration. Whether they produce one chip or one million, this cost remains static.

2. Variable Overhead Variable overhead fluctuates in total in direct proportion to changes in the activity level, but remains constant on a per-unit basis.

Classical Examples: Indirect materials (lubricants, glue), indirect labor (overtime premiums), and electricity for production equipment.

2026 Context: Variable overhead now includes "digital consumables."

Example: A cloud-native app developer pays for server "compute credits" based on traffic. If user activity doubles, the server cooling and electricity costs (billed to the company) double. This is a pure variable overhead.

The "Step-Fixed" Reality

Many modern overheads are actually step-fixed. A customer service AI chatbot might handle 10,000 queries for a flat fee. The moment volume hits 10,001, the company must upgrade to the next tier of processing power, causing a "step" jump in costs. Management accountants in 2026 must be vigilant in identifying these break points to avoid budget shocks.

3b. Corporate vs. Departmental Overhead

Distinguishing between corporate and departmental overhead is critical for performance evaluation. It separates costs a manager can control from those they cannot.

Departmental Overhead (Traceable)

These are costs incurred specifically for the benefit of a single department. If the department were eliminated, these costs would disappear.

Controllability: The department manager usually has high control over these costs.

Examples:

Supplies: Solder used specifically in the Assembly Department.

Supervision: The salary of the foreman supervising the Finishing Department.

Tech: A specialized 3D printing software license used only by the R&D team.

Corporate Overhead (Common/Allocated)

These are costs incurred for the benefit of the organization as a whole. They are often referred to as "common costs."

The Challenge: Allocating these costs to departments can be arbitrary and often leads to friction between division managers.

2026 Trends:

The "Headquarters" Tax: Corporate HQ often provides legal, HR, and strategic services. In 2026, with remote work, "Corporate" overhead also includes the cost of the virtual collaboration platforms (e.g., Enterprise Metaverse environments) used by all staff.

ESG Reporting Costs: The cost of producing a company-wide Sustainability Report is a corporate overhead. Allocating this to specific departments requires sophisticated tracking of which departments contributed most to the carbon footprint.

Strategic Insight: A common mistake is allocating corporate overhead based on revenue. This punishes high-performing departments effectively taxing their success.

2026 best practices suggest allocating corporate costs based on service usage (e.g., allocating HR costs based on headcount, not revenue).

3c. Determination of Allocation Base

The Allocation Base (or Cost Driver) is the denominator used to assign overhead costs to products. The accuracy of product costing depends almost entirely on choosing the correct base.

The Evolution of the Base

Traditional (Pre-2000): Direct Labor Hours (DLH) or Direct Labor Dollars.

Why it failed: In automated factories, labor is a tiny fraction of cost. Using DLH to allocate millions in overhead leads to distorted product costs.

Modern (2010-2020): Machine Hours or Material Costs.

Better for manufacturing, but still lacks precision for service industries.

Advanced (2026 & Beyond): Activity Drivers and Data-Driven Metrics.

2026 Allocation Drivers

In the era of Industry 5.0, allocation bases have become highly granular, often captured automatically by IoT (Internet of Things) sensors.

Overhead Cost Pool	Traditional Base	2026 Advanced Base (Driver)
Machine Maintenance	Machine Hours	Vibration/Heat Anomalies (IoT Sensor Data)

Quality Control Number of Inspections AI Vision Scans (Number of items scanned)
Purchasing Dept Number of Orders Vendor Complexity Score (Rating of difficulty)
ESG/Carbon Tax Square Footage Kilowatt-hours (kWh) Consumed
Cloud Server Costs Headcount API Calls / Compute Cycles

The Plant-Wide vs. Departmental Rate Dilemma

Plant-Wide Rate: One single rate for the whole factory. Simple, but inaccurate. It assumes all products consume overhead resources evenly.

Departmental Rates: Separate rates for "Machining" (machine-hour driven) and "Assembly" (labor-hour driven). This is the standard for the CMA exam. It acknowledges that different departments have different cost drivers.

3d. Allocation of Service Department Costs

Service departments (Support Departments) provide essential backing to Operating Departments (Production) but do not generate revenue directly. Examples include IT, HR, Maintenance, and Cafeteria.

To determine the true cost of a product, the costs of these service departments must be allocated to the operating departments. There are three recognized methods, ranging from simple to mathematically precise.

Method 1: The Direct Method

This is the most widely used method due to its simplicity.

Process: Allocates service department costs only to operating departments. It completely ignores services provided by one service department to another.

Flaw: If the Power Plant provides electricity to the Maintenance Shop, the Direct Method ignores this cost interaction.

Verdict: Acceptable for external reporting, but poor for internal managerial decision-making.

Method 2: The Step-Down (Sequential) Method

This method recognizes that service departments support each other, but only in one direction.

Process:

Rank service departments (usually by the highest dollar amount of service provided to others).

Allocate the first service department's costs to all other departments (service and operating).

"Close" that department. It cannot receive any costs back.

Move to the next service department and repeat.

Benefit: More accurate than Direct Method.

Flaw: It is one-way. It does not account for the "feedback loop" (e.g., IT supports HR, and HR supports IT).

Method 3: The Reciprocal Method

This is the most theoretically accurate method.

Process: It recognizes mutual services completely. It uses simultaneous linear equations (or matrix algebra) to solve for the true cost of each service department before allocation.

2026 Relevance: Historically, this was avoided because the math was "hard." In 2026, with AI-driven ERP systems (like SAP S/4HANA or Oracle Cloud), the Reciprocal Method is executed instantly in the background. The CMA exam requires candidates to understand the logic (simultaneous equations) even if software does the heavy lifting.

Hypothetical Financial Transaction & Problem Solving

To demonstrate the application of these concepts, we will look at a scenario involving "QuantuMech Robotics," a manufacturer of medical droids.
The Scenario

QuantuMech Robotics has two Service Departments and two Production Departments.

Service Dept 1: IT & AI Support (InfoSys) - Maintains the robotic assembly code.

Service Dept 2: Facilities (Facil) - Manages power and cleaning.

Production Dept 1: Fabrication (Fab) - Cuts and molds metal.

Production Dept 2: Assembly (Assem) - Wires and finishes the droids.

Budgeted Overhead Costs (2026):

InfoSys: $600,000

Facilities: $800,000

Usage Data (Allocation Base):

InfoSys costs are allocated based on Support Tickets.

Facilities costs are allocated based on Square Footage.

User Department	Support Tickets (InfoSys Driver)	Square Footage (Facilities Driver)
InfoSys	N/A	2,000
Facilities	200	N/A
Fabrication	600	10,000
Assembly	1,200	8,000
TOTAL	2,000	20,000

The Problem

Required: Allocate the service department costs to the Production Departments (Fabrication and Assembly) using the Step-Down Method.

Note: Allocate Facilities first, as it provides a broader base of service (physical space) to the organization.

The Solution

Step 1: Allocate Facilities Costs We allocate the $800,000 Facilities cost to InfoSys, Fabrication, and Assembly based on Square Footage.

Total Square Footage used by recipients: 2,000 (InfoSys)+10,000 (Fab)+8,000 (Assem)=20,000 sq ft

Allocation Ratios:

To InfoSys: 2,000/20,000=10%

To Fab: 10,000/20,000=50%

To Assem: 8,000/20,000=40%

Cost Distribution:

InfoSys receives: 10%×$800,000=$80,000

Fab receives: 50%×$800,000=$400,000

Assem receives: 40%×$800,000=$320,000

Step 2: Allocate InfoSys Costs (The Step-Down) Now we must allocate InfoSys.

Original Cost: $600,000

Add Allocation from Facilities: + $80,000

New Total to Allocate: $680,000

Crucial Rule: Under Step-Down, we cannot allocate back to Facilities. We only allocate forward to Production (Fab and Assem).

Relevant Driver (Support Tickets):

Fab: 600 tickets

Assem: 1,200 tickets

Note: We ignore the 200 tickets from Facilities because Facilities is "closed."

New Total Base: 600+1,200=1,800 tickets

Allocation Ratios:

To Fab: 600/1,800=33.33% (approx 1/3)

To Assem: 1,200/1,800=66.67% (approx 2/3)

Cost Distribution:

Fab receives: (600/1,800)×$680,000=$226,667

Assem receives: (1,200/1,800)×$680,000=$453,333

Final Total Allocated Overhead:

Department	Allocated from Facilities	Allocated from InfoSys	Total Allocated Overhead
Fabrication	$400,000	$226,667	$626,667
Assembly	$320,000	$453,333	$773,333
Total	$720,000	$680,000	$1,400,000

(Check: The total original cost was $600k + $800k = $1.4M. The total allocated is $1.4M. The math holds.)

Conclusion and Strategic Next Step

In 2026, the mechanical calculation of overhead (like the Step-Down method above) is handled by AI agents. The role of the CMA is to audit the drivers. A CMA must ask: Is "Square Footage" really the best driver for Facilities costs in a highly digital, remote-work environment? Perhaps "Energy Consumption" or "Headcount" would be more equitable.

The future of overhead management lies not in the math, but in the judgment used to select the parameters that the AI uses.

A. Lean Resource Management Techniques

Lean is often misunderstood as simply "cost-cutting." In reality, Lean is a philosophy of value creation through the relentless elimination of waste (Muda). For a CMA in 2026, "Lean" means doing more with less, but doing it smarter, not just harder.

1. The Core Philosophy: Value vs. Waste

At its heart, Lean asks one simple question: Would the customer pay for this specific action? If the answer is no, it is waste.

Traditionally, we categorized waste into seven types (TIMWOOD):

Transportation: Moving goods unnecessarily.

Inventory: Holding excess stock (cash tied up on shelves).

Motion: Unnecessary movement of people (e.g., walking to find tools).

Waiting: Idle time due to bottlenecks.

Overproduction: Making more than demanded (the "sin of sins" in Lean).

Over-processing: Adding features the customer didn't ask for.

Defects: Errors that require rework.

In 2026, we add an 8th waste: Unutilized Talent. This is when a human employee does robotic work (like data entry) that an AI agent could do, preventing them from doing creative problem-solving.

2. Key Techniques & Their 2026 Evolution

a. Just-in-Time (JIT) in an Era of Disruption

Traditional View: JIT involves receiving goods only as they are needed in the production process, reducing inventory costs to near zero.

2026 CMA Update: The post-pandemic world taught us that "zero inventory" is dangerous if a supply chain breaks. In 2026, JIT has evolved into "Just-in-Time, Just-in-Case."

Example: An automotive manufacturer in Detroit used to hold 2 hours of steel inventory. Now, using Predictive AI, they hold 2 hours of standard inventory but automatically buffer up to 2 days' worth if the AI detects a potential strike or weather event in the supplier's region. It is calculated risk, not blind minimalism.

b. Kaizen (Continuous Improvement)

Traditional View: Small, incremental changes made by employees to improve efficiency.

2026 CMA Update: We now see Digital Kaizen. Instead of a suggestion box, shop floor workers wear AR (Augmented Reality) glasses that capture data. If a worker struggles to assemble a part, the system flags it. The "improvement" is then simulated in a Digital Twin (a virtual replica of the factory) before being rolled out physically.

c. The 5S Framework

This is the housekeeping of Lean, essential for safety and efficiency:

Sort (Seiri): Remove unneeded items.

Set in Order (Seiton): A place for everything.

Shine (Seiso): Clean the workspace to spot defects (oil leaks are visible on a clean floor).

Standardize (Seiketsu): Create rules for the first three.

Sustain (Shitsuke): Self-discipline to keep it up.

2026 Note: In modern offices, 5S applies to Data Hygiene. "Sorting" now means archiving old data so your AI analytics run faster. "Shining" means cleansing datasets of errors so your forecasts are accurate.

3. Kanban Systems

Kanban is a visual signaling system. In a factory, when a bin of bolts is empty, a card (Kanban) is sent upstream to request more.

Real-world Example: Imagine a supermarket shelf. When you buy the last carton of milk, a sensor detects the empty space. In 2026, this is e-Kanban. The sensor doesn't just alert the back room; it signals the dairy farm's distribution center 50 miles away, automatically triggering a delivery drone or truck without a human manager ever making a phone call.

B. Enterprise Resource Planning (ERP)

If Lean is the philosophy, ERP is the central nervous system. An ERP system integrates all the distinct functions of a business—finance, HR, supply chain, sales—into a single, flowing source of truth.

1. The Shift to "Composable" ERP

For decades, companies bought massive, monolithic ERP suites (like SAP or Oracle) that did everything but were hard to change.

The 2026 Reality: The trend is Composable ERP. This means businesses buy "best-of-breed" modules and connect them via APIs. You might use one vendor for Finance, another for HR, and a specialized AI tool for Supply Chain planning.

Why this matters for CMAs: You need to understand integration costs and data governance. If the Finance module doesn't "speak" the same language as the Inventory module, your cost accounting will be wrong.

2. Core Modules and Financial Implications

a. Financial Management Module

This is the heart of the beast. It collects data from everywhere else to produce the General Ledger.

Function: Automates accounts payable/receivable, fixed asset management, and cash flow analysis.

2026 Feature: Continuous Close. Instead of waiting until the end of the month to close the books, AI agents reconcile transactions in real-time. A CMA can see the exact P&L (Profit and Loss) status on Tuesday at 2 PM, rather than waiting for the "month-end close" two weeks later.

b. Supply Chain Management (SCM) Module

Function: Manages procurement, order management, and logistics.

2026 Feature: Blockchain Integration. For high-value items (like pharmaceuticals or luxury goods), the ERP records every movement on a blockchain. This proves authenticity and ethical sourcing (ESG compliance), which is now a major part of the CMA Part 2 exam (Strategic Financial Management).

c. Human Capital Management (HCM) Module

Function: Payroll, benefits, and performance.

2026 Feature: Skills-Based Planning. The ERP analyzes the workforce not just by "Job Title" but by "Skill Set." If a new product line requires Python coding, the ERP scans the entire employee base to find hidden talent before suggesting expensive new hires.

3. Risks and Controls in ERP

As a CMA, you are the guardian of Internal Controls.

The "Black Box" Risk: With AI making decisions (e.g., automatically reordering $1M of stock), how do we know it's right?

The Solution: We implement "Human-in-the-loop" controls. The ERP can automate orders up to $10,000, but anything above that triggers a workflow requiring a human manager's digital signature.

C. Capacity Management and Analysis

Capacity management is the science of balancing Demand (what customers want) with Supply (what we can produce). It is arguably the most mathematical part of the CMA curriculum.

1. The Theory of Constraints (TOC)

Developed by Eliyahu Goldratt, TOC is crucial for the CMA exam. It states that every system has at least one constraint (bottleneck) that limits its total output.

The Analogy: Imagine a hiking troop. The troop can only move as fast as the slowest hiker (the bottleneck). If the fastest hikers run ahead, the group breaks apart (inventory builds up).

The 5 Focusing Steps:

Identify the constraint (Find the slow machine).

Exploit the constraint (Ensure the slow machine never stops; give it the best workers).

Subordinate everything else (Run other machines only at the speed of the bottleneck).

Elevate the constraint (Buy a second machine).

Repeat (Find the new bottleneck).

2. Capacity Planning Strategies

Companies must decide when to add capacity. This is a strategic financial decision.

a. Lead Strategy (Aggressive)

Concept: Add capacity before demand increases.

Pros: You never lose a sale; you can capture market share quickly.

Cons: High risk. If demand doesn't come, you have expensive idle machines.

Example: A tech company building a massive server farm in 2025, betting that AI demand will triple in 2026.

b. Lag Strategy (Conservative)

Concept: Add capacity only after the facility is running at 100% full.

Pros: High ROI (Return on Investment); minimal risk of waste.

Cons: You will lose customers during the wait; poor service levels.

Example: A popular restaurant that only opens a second location after there are lines out the door every night for a year.

c. Match Strategy (Moderate)

Concept: Add small amounts of capacity frequently to track demand.

2026 Context: This is now the most popular strategy due to Scalable Cloud Manufacturing. Companies use 3D printing and flexible contracts to "burst" capacity up or down by 10% month-to-month, avoiding the "all or nothing" risks of the past.

3. Throughput Accounting

Standard cost accounting (allocating overheads) can be misleading in capacity analysis. The CMA exam emphasizes Throughput Accounting:
$Throughput = SalesRevenue - TrulyVariableCosts(Materials)$

Rule: In the short term, labor and overhead are often fixed. Therefore, you should maximize Throughput per unit of the Constraint.

Scenario: If Machine A is the bottleneck, you don't produce the product with the highest profit margin; you produce the product that generates the most profit per minute of Machine A time.

Hypothetical Financial Transaction & Problem Solving

Let's apply this "2026 CMA" knowledge to a rigorous problem involving Capacity and Throughput Accounting.
Scenario: The "GreenChip" Decision

Company: Apex Semiconductors Inc. Year: 2026 Situation: Apex manufactures two types of AI chips: the Standard AI (high volume) and the Pro AI (high complexity). The factory is running at full capacity. The bottleneck is the Lithography Machine, which has only 2,000 hours available next month.

Data Table:

Metric	Standard AI Chip	Pro AI Chip
Selling Price	$150	$400
Direct Materials	$60	$120
Variable Overhead	$10	$20
Lithography Time (Bottleneck)	0.5 hours	2.0 hours
Maximum Market Demand	3,000 units	1,000 units

The Problem: The Marketing Manager wants to push the Pro AI chip because it has a higher profit margin per unit. The Production Manager argues they should focus on the Standard AI. Question: As the CMA, what is the optimal production mix to maximize profits, and what is the total Throughput?

The Solution

Step 1: Calculate Throughput per Unit We ignore fixed costs (like rent or supervisor salaries) because they won't change based on this decision. We look at Throughput Contribution.

Throughput=SellingPrice−TotallyVariableCosts(Materials+VariableOH)

Standard AI: $150 - ($60 + $10) = $80 per unit.

Pro AI: $400 - ($120 + $20) = $260 per unit.

Initial thought: The Marketing Manager looks right! The Pro AI makes $260 vs. $80. But wait—we have a constraint.

Step 2: Calculate Throughput per Constraint Hour We must analyze how much money we make for every hour the bottleneck machine runs.

Standard AI: $$$80 \div 0.5 \text{ hours} = \textbf{$160 per hour}$$

Pro AI: $$$260 \div 2.0 \text{ hours} = \textbf{$130 per hour}$$

Analysis: The Standard AI is actually more profitable because it uses the scarce resource (Lithography time) more efficiently. Every hour spent on Standard chips generates $160, while Pro chips only generate $130.

Step 3: Determine Production Mix We prioritize the product with the highest Throughput per Constraint Hour (Standard AI).

Prioritize Standard AI:

Demand: 3,000 units.

Time required:
3,000×0.5 hours=1,500 hours.

We have 2,000 hours available, so we can make all of them.

Remaining Hours:
2,000−1,500=500 hours.

Fill remaining capacity with Pro AI:

We have 500 hours left.

Time per unit: 2.0 hours.

Possible production:
500÷2.0=250 units.

(Demand is 1,000, but we can only make 250).

Step 4: Calculate Total Throughput

Standard AI:
3,000 units×$80=$240,000

Pro AI:
250 units×$260=$65,000

Total Throughput: $305,000

Step 5: The "2026 Strategic" Twist (ESG) Hypothetical addition: Suppose the Standard AI chip uses a material that will be banned by new 2027 ESG regulations, potentially devaluing the inventory. A CMA might advise reducing Standard production slightly to avoid "stranded asset" risk, even if the math says it's more profitable today. This is the qualitative judgment tested in the essay section of the CMA exam.

Conclusion

In 2026, Supply Chain Management is no longer about isolated silos of "buying," "making," and "shipping." It is a dynamic ecosystem where Lean principles drive efficiency, ERP systems provide the digital backbone, and Capacity Management dictates the rhythm of profitability.

For you, the aspiring CMA, the key takeaway is integration. You cannot optimize capacity without understanding the ERP data that feeds it. You cannot implement Lean without understanding the financial throughput it generates. The future belongs to those who can speak the languages of both operations and finance fluently.

a. Value Chain Analysis: Beyond the Factory Floor

In the classic textbooks, Michael Porter's Value Chain was a linear diagram: raw materials came in, widgets got made, and products went out. In 2026, the value chain is no longer linear; it is a digital, circular ecosystem.

The Core Concept Value chain analysis identifies every step a business takes to create a product or service and asks a brutal question: Does this step add value to the customer, or does it just add cost? It breaks the organization into Primary Activities (Inbound Logistics, Operations, Outbound Logistics, Marketing/Sales, Service) and Support Activities (Procurement, HR, Tech Development, Infrastructure).

The 2026 Evolution: "Total Value" and ESG Today, you cannot perform a value chain analysis without overlaying Environmental, Social, and Governance (ESG) data.

Inbound Logistics: It's not just about getting steel to the factory cheapest. It's about "Scope 3 emissions." For example, a car manufacturer in 2026 tracks the carbon footprint of the shipping vessel bringing lithium batteries from overseas. If the logistics are cheap but carbon-heavy, the value is eroded by regulatory fines and reputational damage.

Operations: This is where Physical AI comes in. In a modern bakery, sensors don't just bake bread; they adjust oven temperatures in real-time based on the humidity of the flour batch to prevent waste. That is value chain optimization—reducing the "cost of poor quality" before it happens.

Marketing & Sales: The value chain now includes "hyper-personalization." A streaming service doesn't just sell subscriptions; it uses generative AI to create custom artwork for movie thumbnails based on a user's viewing history. This personalized touch creates immense value at a near-zero marginal cost.

Real-World Application Consider a global coffee chain. In the past, their value chain analysis focused on buying cheap beans (Procurement) and roasting them efficiently (Operations).

2026 Analysis: They realize their customers value ethical sourcing more than a $0.20 price drop. The "value" has shifted upstream. They invest in blockchain technology to track the beans from the farmer to the cup. This is a "Support Activity" (Technology Development) that drastically increases the value of the "Primary Activity" (Sales), allowing them to charge a premium.

b. Value-Added Concepts: The Ruthless Elimination of Waste

To be a successful management accountant, you must develop a specific kind of vision: you must look at a process and see the "fat." Every activity in a business falls into one of two buckets: Value-Added (VA) or Non-Value-Added (NVA).

1. Value-Added (VA) Activities These are activities that the customer is willing to pay for. They transform the product or service in a way that meets a customer need.

Example: A carpenter sanding a table is adding value; the wood is becoming smoother, which the customer wants.

Example: A software engineer coding a new feature for an app is adding value; the user gets a new capability.

2. Non-Value-Added (NVA) Activities These are pure waste. The customer does not care about them and would not pay for them if they had a choice.

Example: Moving the table from one side of the factory to the other because of a bad layout. The customer doesn't care if the table traveled 500 feet; they just want the table.

Example: A loan officer re-entering data into a spreadsheet because two software systems don't talk to each other. This is "data friction."

3. Business Value-Added (BVA) This is the tricky middle ground. The customer doesn't care about these, but the business must do them to survive or comply with laws.

Example: Filing tax returns. A customer buying a shoe doesn't care if Nike filed its taxes, but if Nike doesn't file, Nike shuts down.

Example: Cybersecurity audits. The customer doesn't "enjoy" the audit, but it protects their data.

The 2026 Shift: AI as the Waste Hunter In 2026, we don't just guess which steps are NVA. We use Process Mining. Imagine a software tool that tracks every click and keystroke of an accounts payable team. It reveals that 40% of the team's time is spent opening email attachments to find invoice numbers.

Solution: Deploy an AI agent to automatically scrape the invoices. The "opening email" step (NVA) is eliminated. The human moves to "analyzing discrepancies" (VA).

c. Process Analysis, Redesign, and Standardization

Once you have identified the waste, you have to fix it. This is where we move from diagnosis to surgery.

Process Analysis: The Digital Twin Before we change a process, we must understand it. In 2026, leading companies use Digital Twins. This is a virtual replica of a business process.

Example: A logistics company creates a digital twin of its warehouse. They run a simulation: "What happens if we switch to autonomous forklifts?" The simulation shows a potential bottleneck at the loading dock that human managers hadn't foreseen. They fix the process in the computer before spending a dime in the real world.

Process Redesign (Business Process Reengineering - BPR) BPR is not about "tweaking"; it is about "obliterating" the old way and starting fresh.

Old Way: You fill out a form, print it, sign it, scan it, and email it to HR.

Redesign: You click one button on your phone. The system uses biometric authentication (FaceID) to sign and automatically updates the database. The intermediate steps are gone.

2026 Context: BPR often involves Geopatriation strategies—redesigning supply chains to move production closer to home (nearshoring) to reduce geopolitical risk, rather than just chasing the lowest labor cost.

Standardization: The SOPs of the Future Standardization reduces variance. If five accountants calculate depreciation five different ways, you have chaos.

Interactive SOPs: In 2026, Standard Operating Procedures (SOPs) aren't dusty binders. They are augmented reality (AR) overlays. A technician fixing a wind turbine wears smart glasses. The glasses highlight the exact bolt to turn and display the torque setting. This standardizes the repair process across thousands of technicians globally, ensuring 100% consistency.

d. Continuous Improvement Concepts

Continuous improvement (CI) is the philosophy that "good enough is never enough." It is not a project with an end date; it is a culture.

The Methodologies

Kaizen (Change for Better): Small, incremental daily changes.

Example: A hotel housekeeping team realizes that keeping the vacuum cleaner on the second floor saves 10 minutes of elevator time per day. Over a year, that's huge savings.

Lean: Focuses on flow and speed by removing waste (Muda).

Example: A hospital uses Lean to reduce the time from "patient arrival" to "doctor consultation" by removing redundant paperwork at the front desk.

Six Sigma: Focuses on quality and consistency by reducing defects to 3.4 per million opportunities.

Example: A chip manufacturer uses statistical analysis to ensure that the thickness of a silicon wafer never deviates by more than a nanometer.

Theory of Constraints (TOC): Focuses on the bottleneck. A chain is only as strong as its weakest link.

Example: An airport realizes the security check is the bottleneck. Adding more check-in counters (non-bottleneck) won't help. They must focus all improvements on the security line.

The 2026 Evolution: Agile & AI The modern twist is Agile integration. Finance teams now work in "sprints." Instead of a massive annual budget process (which is obsolete by the time it's finished), they do "rolling forecasts" updated every two weeks.

Example: A software company releases updates every Friday. The customer support team reviews the feedback on Monday (Check), improves the help scripts on Tuesday (Act), and trains the chatbots on Wednesday (Plan/Do). This is the PDCA (Plan-Do-Check-Act) cycle at digital speed.

e. Benchmarking and Best Practice Analysis

Benchmarking is the art of humility. It admits: "Someone else is doing this better than us. Let's learn from them."

Types of Benchmarking

Competitive Benchmarking: Comparing yourself to direct rivals.

Example: Burger King timing the drive-thru speed of McDonald's to see if they are lagging.

Internal Benchmarking: Comparing different departments within your own company.

Example: A bank notices its New York branch processes loans 30% faster than its London branch. They analyze the New York process and copy it to London.

Functional/Generic Benchmarking: Comparing a specific function to the best in the world, regardless of industry.

Example: A hospital wants to improve patient admission speed. They don't look at other hospitals; they look at Formula 1 pit crews or Marriott Hotels. They ask: "How do they check people in so fast?"

The 2026 Evolution: Real-Time Data In 2026, benchmarking is no longer an annual retrospective. It is real-time.

Data Coalitions: Companies now subscribe to anonymized data pools (like APQC or industry-specific DAOs). A CFO can log in on Tuesday morning and see that their "Days Sales Outstanding" (DSO) is 45 days, while the industry top-quartile average just dropped to 38 days due to new AI billing tools. The feedback loop is instant.

f. Cost of Quality (COQ) Analysis

This is a critical area for the CMA exam. Quality is not free, but poor quality is much more expensive. COQ measures the financial impact of quality activities.

The Four Categories (PAF Model)

Prevention Costs (Investments to keep defects from happening):

Definition: Money spent before production begins.

Examples: Employee training, quality engineering, preventive maintenance on machines, choosing higher-quality suppliers.

2026 Trend: Investing in "Predictive Maintenance" AI that listens to the vibrations of a machine and orders a replacement part before the gear snaps.

Appraisal Costs (Detecting defects before shipping):

Definition: Inspection and testing.

Examples: Quality control inspectors, lab testing, software code reviews, calibration of measuring equipment.

Note: As Prevention goes up, Appraisal can often go down because you trust the process more.

Internal Failure Costs (Defects found BEFORE the customer sees them):

Definition: The product is broken, but it's still in the factory.

Examples: Scrap (throwing it away), Rework (fixing it), downtime due to broken machines, re-testing.

Cost: Expensive, but at least the reputation is safe.

External Failure Costs (Defects found BY the customer):

Definition: The nightmare scenario. The product failed in the field.

Examples: Warranty claims, product recalls, lawsuits, lost sales, damaged brand reputation, customer support center costs.

Cost: The most expensive category. A $10 part that fails in a customer's hand can cost millions in lost brand equity.

The "Hidden" Costs of Quality Modern analysis also looks at Sustainability Failure Costs. If a company produces excess waste that isn't "defective" product but is "environmental" waste, they pay in carbon taxes and cleanup fees. This is now part of the COQ equation.
Hypothetical Financial Transaction & Problem Solving

Scenario: "ElectroDrive Motors Inc."

Background: ElectroDrive manufactures electric scooter motors. In 2025, they faced a crisis: customers were returning motors because of a "whining noise" caused by a misalignment of the internal magnet. This is an External Failure.

Management decides to implement a new 2026 Quality Initiative.

They will install an AI-driven laser alignment system (Prevention Cost).

They will hire a specialized quality engineer to oversee the AI (Prevention Cost).

They will reduce manual inspections because the AI is more accurate (Savings in Appraisal Cost).

The Financial Data (Annualized):

Current Situation (2025):

Manual Inspection Labor: $200,000

Scrap (Motors thrown away during production): $150,000

Warranty Claims (Returns & Repairs): $450,000

Lost Sales due to Bad Reviews (Estimated): $300,000

Proposed Situation (2026 Forecast):

Lease cost of AI Laser System: $80,000 / year

Salary for AI Quality Engineer: $120,000 / year

Manual Inspection Labor: Reduces by 70%.

Scrap: Reduces by 60% (Lasers catch issues early enough to fix cheaply).

Warranty Claims: Reduces by 90%.

Lost Sales: Reduces by 80% (Reputation recovers).

Problem:

Calculate the Total Cost of Quality (COQ) for the Current Situation (2025).

Calculate the Total Cost of Quality (COQ) for the Proposed Situation (2026).

Determine the Net Financial Benefit (or Loss) of the new initiative.

Identify which COQ categories increased and which decreased.

Solution & Explanation

Step 1: Calculate Current COQ (2025)

Prevention: $0 (None mentioned)

Appraisal: $200,000 (Manual Inspection)

Internal Failure: $150,000 (Scrap)

External Failure: $450,000 (Warranty) + $300,000 (Lost Sales) = $750,000

Total Current COQ: $0 + $200,000 + $150,000 + $750,000 = $1,100,000

Step 2: Calculate Proposed COQ (2026)

Prevention:

AI System Lease: $80,000

Engineer Salary: $120,000

Total Prevention: $200,000

Appraisal:

Current ($200,000) reduced by 70% means 30% remains.

$200,000 * 0.30 = $60,000

Internal Failure:

Current ($150,000) reduced by 60% means 40% remains.

$150,000 * 0.40 = $60,000

External Failure:

Warranty ($450,000) reduced by 90% means 10% remains = $45,000.

Lost Sales ($300,000) reduced by 80% means 20% remains = $60,000.

Total External: $45,000 + $60,000 = $105,000

Total Proposed COQ: $200,000 + $60,000 + $60,000 + $105,000 = $425,000

Step 3: Determine Net Financial Benefit

Savings = Current COQ - Proposed COQ

$1,100,000 - $425,000 = $675,000

Step 4: Analysis of Trade-offs

Prevention Costs increased significantly (from $0 to $200,000).

Appraisal Costs decreased (from $200,000 to $60,000).

Failure Costs (Internal + External) plummeted (from $900,000 to $165,000).

Conclusion: This is a textbook example of the 1-10-100 Rule. Spending $1 on Prevention often saves $10 in Correction and $100 in Failure. By shifting funds into Prevention (the AI system), ElectroDrive not only saved $675,000 annually but also protected its brand equity, which is vital for long-term survival in the competitive EV market of 2026.

Conclusion: The Strategic Partner

As we look toward 2026 and beyond, the role of the management accountant has fundamentally changed. We are no longer scorekeepers; we are coaches. Whether it is utilizing Value Chain Analysis to decarbonize a supply chain, employing Digital Twins for process redesign, or calculating the Cost of Quality for an AI investment, the goal remains the same: Value Creation.

The businesses that survive in this era will be the ones that can ruthlessly identify waste, standardize their best practices, and continuously improve at the speed of algorithms. Your job is to provide the financial clarity that makes those decisions possible.

Internal Controls (15% - Levels A, B, and C)

Governance, risk, and compliance

a. Internal Control Structure and Management Philosophy

The foundation of any robust GRC system is the Internal Control Structure. Think of this not as a set of rules, but as the organization's "immune system." It is designed to identify threats (risks) and neutralize them before they harm the company's health (objectives).

For the 2026 CMA, the gold standard remains the COSO Internal Control—Integrated Framework. This framework organizes internal control into five components, but the most critical one is the Control Environment. This is often called the "Tone at the Top."
The Management Philosophy

Management philosophy is the intangible "vibe" that dictates how business is done. It reflects the integrity, ethical values, and competence of the entity's people.

If management is aggressive about hitting earnings targets at any cost, the internal control structure will likely collapse, no matter how many written policies exist. Conversely, a management philosophy that prioritizes transparency and ethical behavior strengthens controls naturally.

Example: Consider a tech startup, "AlphaTech." The CEO believes in "moving fast and breaking things." While this philosophy aids innovation, it often leads to bypassing procurement protocols to buy software quickly. In contrast, a mature bank operates with a philosophy of "trust and verify." Even though the bank moves slower, its management philosophy inherently supports a stronger control structure because every employee knows that bypassing a rule is culturally unacceptable.

In 2026, management philosophy also encompasses Digital Ethics. It's not just about financial fraud anymore; it's about how management views data privacy and AI governance. Does management view customer data as a commodity to be exploited or an asset to be protected? This mindset is part of the control structure.

b. Internal Control Policies for Safeguarding and Assurance

Once the environment is set, we need the actual mechanics: the Control Activities. These are the policies and procedures that help ensure management directives are carried out.

We generally categorize these into three types:

Preventive Controls: Designed to stop an error or fraud before it happens.

Detective Controls: Designed to find an error after it has occurred.

Corrective Controls: Steps taken to fix the error once detected.

Safeguarding Assets

The most traditional goal of internal control is safeguarding assets—cash, inventory, and equipment. However, in the modern era, "assets" also include intellectual property and customer data.

Policies for safeguarding often involve Segregation of Duties (SoD). This is the concept that no single person should be responsible for authorizing a transaction, recording the transaction, and holding custody of the asset.

Example: Imagine a retail chain.

Preventive: The Point of Sale (POS) system requires a manager's fingerprint to void a transaction over $50. This prevents a cashier from fake-voiding a sale and pocketing the cash.

Detective: At the end of the week, the accounting team reconciles the bank deposit slips against the daily sales reports. If there is a discrepancy, the detective control highlights it.

Safeguarding: Inventory is kept in a locked warehouse (physical safeguard), and access is restricted to authorized personnel using biometric scanners (digital safeguard).

Assurance

Assurance is the confidence that financial reports are reliable. Policies here focus on the accuracy of records. This includes Standardized Journal Entry procedures. A policy might state: "All journal entries over $10,000 must be reviewed by the Controller." This provides assurance that large adjustments are valid.

c. Internal Control Risk

Risk is the possibility that an event will occur and adversely affect the achievement of objectives. In auditing and GRC, we view risk through a specific lens.

The Audit Risk Model is essential for CMAs:
$$AuditRisk=InherentRisk\times ControlRisk\times DetectionRisk$$

Inherent Risk: The natural risk associated with an account or industry before any controls are applied. Cash, for instance, has high inherent risk because it is easy to steal. Complex derivatives have high inherent risk because they are hard to value.

Control Risk: The risk that the company's internal controls will fail to prevent or detect a material misstatement. If a company has sloppy password policies, control risk is high.

Detection Risk: The risk that an auditor (internal or external) will fail to catch the error during testing.

The Interplay

You cannot eliminate risk; you can only manage it. If Inherent Risk is high (e.g., a casino handling cash), the company must lower Control Risk by implementing strict cameras and cage procedures.

Example: A pharmaceutical company faces high Inherent Risk in its R&D valuation because estimating the future value of a drug trial is subjective. To mitigate this, they implement a Control: A valuation committee of three independent experts must approve the estimates. If this committee rarely meets or rubber-stamps documents, the Control Risk remains high. Consequently, the auditor must increase their testing to lower the Detection Risk.
d. Testing Methods forInternal Controls

How do we know the controls work? We test them. In 2026, testing methods have moved beyond manual ticking and tying to include data analytics, though traditional methods remain valid.

1. Inquiry and Observation

This is the simplest form. You ask the staff how they do things and watch them do it.

Weakness: People tend to behave perfectly when they know they are being watched (the Hawthorne Effect).

2. Inspection

Reviewing documents for evidence of controls. For example, looking for a physical signature on a purchase order.

3. Re-performance

The auditor re-does the control to see if they get the same result. If the control is a monthly bank reconciliation, the auditor takes the bank statement and the ledger and performs the reconciliation themselves.

4. Walkthroughs

Tracing a transaction from its inception (e.g., receiving a customer order) to its conclusion (e.g., cash hitting the bank account). This confirms the auditor understands the flow of the system.

5. Continuous Monitoring (The 2026 Standard)

Modern ERP systems allow for automated testing. Instead of testing a sample of 25 transactions, AI tools can test 100% of the population.

Example: In a traditional audit, an auditor might randomly select 30 expense reports to check for receipts. In a Continuous Monitoring environment, an algorithm scans every expense report submitted in 2026. It flags duplicate

amounts, round numbers (often a sign of fraud), or expenses claimed on weekends. The human auditor then only investigates the flagged items.
e. Control Deficiency Remediation

When a test fails, it reveals a deficiency. Not all deficiencies are created equal.

Deficiency: A minor shortcoming.

Significant Deficiency: More serious, merits attention by those responsible for oversight.

Material Weakness: A reasonable possibility that a material misstatement will not be prevented or detected.

The Remediation Process

Remediation is the "fix." It involves Root Cause Analysis. You don't just fix the error; you fix the process that allowed the error.

Example: An auditor discovers that a terminated employee still had access to the payroll system (a Deficiency).

Immediate Action: Revoke access.

Root Cause: HR sends termination emails manually, and IT sometimes misses them.

Remediation: Automate the link between the HR portal and the Active Directory. When HR marks an employee as "Terminated," the system automatically locks their user account.

Retesting: After three months, the auditor tests the new automated link to ensure it works.

f. Corporate Governance

Corporate Governance is the system of rules, practices, and processes by which a company is directed and controlled. It involves balancing the interests of a company's many stakeholders: shareholders, management, customers, suppliers, financiers, government, and the community.

The Board of Directors

The Board is the ultimate governing body. In 2026, the CMA curriculum emphasizes the Audit Committee.

The Audit Committee must be composed of independent directors.

At least one member must be a financial expert.

They hire and oversee the external auditors, not management. This ensures the auditors are not afraid to criticize management.

ESG (Environmental, Social, and Governance)

By 2026, Governance is heavily tied to ESG. Governance now includes oversight of climate risk and social equity. A company with poor governance regarding environmental compliance faces massive financial risk from fines and reputation loss.

Example: A clothing manufacturer has a Board that ignores supply chain labor practices. This is a failure of Governance. If a scandal breaks out regarding child labor, the stock price crashes. Good governance would involve a "Social Responsibility Committee" that regularly audits suppliers, thereby reducing risk.

g. External Audit Requirements

External audit provides objective assurance to the public. For public companies in the US, this is governed by the Sarbanes-Oxley Act (SOX) of 2002 and the PCAOB.

The Integrated Audit

Public companies require an Integrated Audit, which provides two opinions:

Opinion on the Financial Statements (Are the numbers accurate?)

Opinion on Internal Control over Financial Reporting (Are the controls effective?)

Audit Opinions

Unqualified (Clean): The best outcome. Everything is fair and accurate.

Qualified: Everything is okay, except for this one specific issue.

Adverse: The financial statements are not fair, or internal controls are ineffective.

Disclaimer: The auditor cannot form an opinion (usually due to lack of records).

Example: If a company calculates revenue differently than GAAP standards require, the external auditor will discuss this with the Audit Committee. If the company refuses to change it, the auditor issues an Adverse Opinion. This usually leads to a massive drop in stock price and SEC investigations.

Hypothetical Financial Transaction & Problem Solving

Let's apply these concepts to a practical scenario relevant to a CMA.

The Scenario

Company: Nebula Logistics (a publicly traded shipping company). Year: 2026. Situation: Nebula Logistics uses a fleet of automated drones for local delivery. The company capitalizes the repair costs of these drones. The Policy: The internal control policy states: "Routine maintenance (oil, battery swaps) should be expensed immediately. Major overhauls that extend the useful life of the drone by more than 1 year should be capitalized." The Transaction: On January 15, 2026, the Maintenance Manager authorizes a payment of $450,000 to "DroneFix Inc." for replacing batteries and rotor blades across the entire fleet. The junior accountant capitalizes this amount as an asset, arguing that new blades make the drones fly better.

The Control Failure

The "Capitalization Review Control" failed. Usually, any capitalization over $100k requires the Controller's signature. The Controller was on vacation, and the Assistant Controller signed it without reviewing the invoice details.

The Problem

Is the accounting treatment correct?

What is the impact on the financial statements if this error is not caught?

Propose the correcting journal entry (assuming the books are still open).

The Solution

Step 1: Analyze the Accounting Treatment According to GAAP, routine maintenance (batteries, rotor blades) maintains the asset's current condition; it does not significantly improve it or extend its life beyond the original estimate. Therefore, this should be an Expense, not an Asset (Capital Expenditure).

Verdict: The accounting is incorrect.

Step 2: Impact Analysis By capitalizing the $450,000 instead of expensing it:

Assets are overstated by $450,000.

Expenses are understated by $450,000.

Net Income is overstated by $450,000 (ignoring tax effects for simplicity).

Retained Earnings (Equity) is overstated.

This is a classic "cookie jar" accounting move (intentional or not) that inflates current profits.

Step 3: Correcting Journal Entry We need to remove the amount from the Asset account (likely "PP&E - Drones") and move it to the Expense account ("Repairs and Maintenance Expense").

Journal Entry:

Date	Account	Debit ($)	Credit ($)
Jan 15, 2026	Repairs and Maintenance Expense	450,000	
	PP&E (Drone Assets)		450,000
	To reclassify erroneous capitalization of routine maintenance.		

Next Steps for the CMA: After booking the entry, the CMA must perform Remediation. The control deficiency was that the Assistant Controller did not understand the difference between CapEx (Capital Expenditure) and OpEx (Operating Expenditure).

Action: Conduct training on capitalization policies.

Action: Update the ERP system to flag any payment to vendors classified as "Maintenance" if the user tries to capitalize it.

Conclusion

Mastering Governance, Risk, and Compliance is about understanding the narrative behind the numbers. For the 2026 CMA, it requires a blend of ethical philosophy, rigid procedural knowledge, and the ability to leverage technology for assurance. Whether it is ensuring a drone repair is expensed correctly or advising the Board on ESG risks, the CMA stands as the gatekeeper of organizational integrity.

2a. General Accounting System Controls

The Foundation of Integrity

Think of General Controls (often called ITGCs - IT General Controls) as the foundation of a house. If the foundation is cracked, it does not matter how secure the locks on the front door (Application Controls) are; the structure is compromised. In 2026, these controls govern the entire IT environment in which your accounting systems live.
Core Components

Organizational Security & Governance: This involves the separation of the IT department from the accounting department. It prevents the people who write the code for the financial software from using the software to process transactions.

Physical Data Center Security: Even in a cloud-first world, physical access matters. This includes biometric locks, mantrap entryways, and surveillance logs for server rooms.

Systems Development Life Cycle (SDLC): When accounting software is updated, it must go through rigorous testing. We use a three-tier environment: Development (writing code), Testing (verifying code), and Production (live data). Code never moves directly from Development to Production.

2026 Trend - AI Governance: General controls now include "Model Risk Management." If an AI is estimating bad debt reserves, we must control who can tweak the algorithm's parameters.

Real-World Examples

Segregation of Duties (SoD): A programmer at a fintech company has access to the source code of the payroll system. General controls ensure this programmer cannot access the live production database to artificially inflate their own salary.

Logical Access via Zero Trust: Instead of a simple password, accessing the General Ledger now requires a "Zero Trust" verification—checking the user's identity, device health, and location every single time they log in.

2b. Application and Transaction Controls

The Gatekeepers of Data

If General Controls are the building's foundation, Application Controls are the specific locks, cameras, and sensors inside the rooms. These are automated procedures embedded within software (like SAP, Oracle, or NetSuite) to ensure that the data entering the system is valid, complete, and accurate.

We categorize these into three distinct phases: Input, Processing, and Output.
1. Input Controls (The Most Critical Phase)

"Garbage in, garbage out." Input controls prevent errors before they enter the system.

Validity Checks: The system compares the entered data against a master file. For example, if you enter a Vendor ID "V-999," the system checks the Vendor Master File. If "V-999" doesn't exist, the transaction is rejected.

Field Checks: Ensures the characters entered are the proper type. A "Date" field should not accept alphabetic characters.

Limit/Range Checks: A payroll system might have a limit check of $10,000 per week. If a clerk accidentally adds a zero and tries to pay someone $50,000, the system automatically flags it.

2. Processing Controls

These ensure data remains intact while it is being calculated or moved.

Run-to-Run Totals: If the "Accounts Payable" module sends a batch of invoices to the "General Ledger" module, the total dollar amount in both systems must match exactly.

Sequence Checks: The system verifies that document numbers (like check numbers or invoice numbers) are sequential. A missing number triggers an audit flag.

3. Output Controls

These ensure the final result is correct and only viewed by authorized eyes.

Distribution Logs: Confidential financial statements are watermarked and their distribution is tracked digitally.

Authentic Scenario

The "Fat Finger" Error: A junior accountant at a logistics firm attempts to pay an invoice for $5,000 but accidentally types $50,000.

Control Activation: The ERP system triggers a Limit Check. A pop-up appears: "Value exceeds authorized threshold of $10,000. Supervisor approval required." The error is stopped before cash leaves the bank.

2c. Technology Controls

The Armor Against Cyber Threats

In the 2026 syllabus, Technology Controls focus on network defense and infrastructure protection. The boundaries of the corporate network have dissolved due to remote work; thus, controls must travel with the data.

Key Defense Mechanisms

Firewalls and Intrusion Prevention Systems (IPS): These filter traffic entering the network. Modern "Next-Gen" firewalls use AI to detect behavioral anomalies, not just known viruses.

Encryption (At Rest and In Transit):

In Transit: When data moves from your laptop to the cloud, it travels through an encrypted tunnel (SSL/TLS).

At Rest: Even if a hacker steals the physical hard drive from a server, the data is scrambled and unreadable without the decryption key.

Endpoint Security: Every laptop and mobile device connecting to the financial system has "Endpoint Detection and Response" (EDR) software that creates a sandbox to contain potential malware.

2026 Context: Quantum Readiness

Financial institutions are now preparing for "Post-Quantum Cryptography." As quantum computers become powerful enough to break traditional encryption, technology controls are shifting toward quantum-resistant algorithms to protect long-term financial secrets.

Shutterstock
2d. Backup Controls

The Safety Net

Backup controls ensure that when (not if) a system fails or is attacked, data can be restored. The gold standard has evolved from simple tape backups to complex, immutable cloud architectures.
The "3-2-1" Rule (Updated for 2026)

- Keep 3 copies of your data.
- Store them on 2 different types of media (e.g., local SSD and Cloud Object Storage).
- Keep 1 copy Immutable and offsite.

Types of Backup Strategies

- Grandfather-Father-Son (GFS): A traditional rotation strategy.
    - Son: Daily backups (kept for a week).
    - Father: Weekly backups (kept for a month).
    - Grandfather: Monthly backups (kept for a year or indefinitely).

Immutable Backups (Ransomware Proofing): This is the most vital control in the 2020s. An immutable backup is "WORM" (Write Once, Read Many). Once written, it cannot be modified or deleted for a set period, even by the system administrator. If ransomware encrypts your live data, it cannot touch the immutable backup.

Verification

A backup is useless if it doesn't work. Recovery Drills are now a quarterly compliance requirement, where teams must prove they can restore a terabyte of financial data within a specific "Recovery Time Objective" (RTO).

2e. Business Continuity Planning (BCP)

Resilience in Chaos

Business Continuity Planning (BCP) is broader than just fixing computers; it is about keeping the business alive. It encompasses Disaster Recovery (DR) but adds the human and operational element.

The BCP Hierarchy

Business Impact Analysis (BIA): Before a disaster, we identify which processes are critical. Payroll might be a "Tier 1" process (must be up in 24 hours), while the marketing blog is "Tier 3" (can wait a week).

Disaster Recovery Plan (DRP): The technical steps to switch servers.

Hot Site: A fully mirrored data center ready to take over instantly. Expensive but zero downtime.

Warm Site: Hardware is ready, but data needs to be loaded. Takes 12-48 hours.

Cold Site: Just a room with power and air conditioning. Equipment must be shipped in.

Crisis Management: Who speaks to the press? Who notifies the investors? BCP defines the chain of command when the CEO is unreachable.

2026 Trend - Operational Resilience: Regulators now demand "Resilience," which assumes failure will happen. It requires firms to have redundant vendors. If the primary cloud provider (e.g., AWS) fails, is there a failover capability to Azure or a private cloud?

Shutterstock

Hypothetical Financial Transaction & Problem Solving

To demonstrate the application of these controls, let us analyze a specific financial scenario involving a procurement fraud attempt.
The Scenario: "The Ghost Vendor"

Date: February 14, 2026 Company: Apex Manufacturing Ltd. Situation: The Accounts Payable (AP) Manager, John, is under financial stress. He decides to create a fake vendor named "J-Services" in the ERP system. He intends to submit a fake invoice for $8,500 (just under the $10,000 approval threshold) for "Consulting Services."

The Transaction:

John logs into the Master Data module.

He enters "J-Services" as a new vendor with his own personal bank account number.

He then logs into the Invoice Processing module.

He enters an invoice for $8,500.

The system attempts to process the payment.

The Problem

Identify the specific control failures that would allow this fraud to succeed, and describe the Preventive Control that should be implemented to stop it.

The Solution

Analysis of Failure: If John succeeds, it indicates a failure in Segregation of Duties (General Control). One person should never have the authority to create a vendor (Master Data) and pay that vendor (Transaction Processing). If the same person can do both, they can pay themselves without oversight.

The Required Control Implementation: To solve this, Apex Manufacturing must implement a strict Three-Way Match combined with Segregation of Duties.

Segregation of Duties (SoD): The ability to "Create/Edit Vendor Master Data" must be restricted to the Purchasing Department, while the ability to "Enter Invoices" is restricted to Accounts Payable. The system permissions should physically prevent John from accessing the "Create Vendor" screen.

System Logic (Application Control):

Step 1: When John tries to create the vendor, the system denies access (Access Control).

Step 2: Even if he bypasses that, when the invoice is entered, the system performs a Validity Check. It looks for a valid Purchase Order (PO) created by an independent purchasing agent. Since "J-Services" provided no goods, there is no receiving report and no PO.

Step 3: The system flags the transaction: "Error: No matching Purchase Order found. Payment blocked."

Outcome: The fraud is prevented not by human oversight, which is fallible, but by hard-coded logic within the application controls.

Technology and Analytics (15% - Levels A, B, and C)

Information systems

1. Accounting Information Systems (AIS)

The Foundation of Financial Truth

Think of the Accounting Information System (AIS) as the digital ledger of a company. It is the specific tool used to collect, store, and process financial and accounting data. Its primary goal is to produce information for decision-makers, auditors, and tax authorities.

In the past, an AIS might have been a physical book. Today, and looking toward 2026, it is a sophisticated software suite that automates the flow of money in and out of the organization.

Getty Images

Core Functions of an AIS

The AIS is designed to handle the "nuts and bolts" of accounting. It typically includes the following subsystems:

Transaction Processing System (TPS): This handles daily events. Every time a sale is made or a bill is paid, the TPS records it.

General Ledger/Financial Reporting System (GL/FRS): This aggregates the data to produce the Balance Sheet, Income Statement, and Cash Flow Statement.

Management Reporting System (MRS): This provides internal reports for management, such as variance analysis and cost reports.

The 2026 Evolution: Automation and Accuracy

By 2026, the entry-level tasks of an AIS have largely been automated. We are seeing a move away from manual data entry toward "Zero-Touch" accounting.

Key features in the 2026 landscape include:

Robotic Process Automation (RPA): Bots now handle repetitive tasks. For example, when an invoice arrives via email, an RPA bot reads it, matches it to a purchase order, and posts it to the ledger without human intervention.

Continuous Auditing: Instead of waiting for the end of the year, the AIS runs continuous checks. If an entry looks suspicious (e.g., a duplicate payment), the system flags it immediately.

Blockchain Integration: For supply chain heavy industries, the AIS verifies transactions against a shared blockchain ledger to ensure the data is immutable and authentic.

Real-World Example: The "Smart" Payable

Imagine a mid-sized logistics company. In the past, a clerk typed invoice numbers into the system. This was prone to error.

Now, the company uses an AIS with Optical Character Recognition (OCR) and AI. A vendor sends a PDF invoice. The AIS "reads" the document. It recognizes the vendor, checks the math, and verifies that the goods were received. If everything matches, the AIS schedules the payment automatically. The accountant only gets involved if there is a discrepancy. This shifts the accountant's job from data entry to exception handling.

2. Enterprise Resource Planning (ERP) Systems

The Central Nervous System

If the AIS is the financial heart, the Enterprise Resource Planning (ERP) system is the brain and nervous system of the entire organization.

An AIS focuses strictly on accounting. An ERP is much broader. It integrates all core business processes into a single system. It ensures that the Finance department, HR, Sales, Manufacturing, and Supply Chain are all looking at the same data at the same time.

How ERP Modules Connect

An ERP is built in "modules." While they serve different departments, they share a single database. This eliminates "data silos" where one department thinks inventory is X, but another thinks it is Y.

Finance Module: (This is essentially the AIS embedded within the ERP).

Supply Chain Management (SCM): Tracks raw materials and logistics.

Human Resources (HR): Manages payroll, hiring, and benefits.

Customer Relationship Management (CRM): Tracks sales leads and customer interactions.

Manufacturing: Monitors production schedules and machine maintenance.

The 2026 Evolution: The Intelligent ERP

For the 2026 CMA, the ERP is no longer just a system of record; it is a system of intelligence.

Cloud-Native Architecture: By 2026, on-premise servers are rare. ERPs exist in the cloud, allowing for real-time updates and remote access from anywhere in the world.

ESG Integration: Modern ERPs now track sustainability metrics. They measure carbon footprints and energy usage alongside financial costs. This is crucial as non-financial reporting becomes mandatory in many jurisdictions.

Predictive Maintenance: The ERP connects to sensors on factory machines (IoT). It can tell the Finance team that a machine will break down next week, allowing them to budget for repairs before the failure happens.

Real-World Example: Inventory Synchronization

Consider a global sneaker manufacturer. Without an ERP, the sales team in New York might sell 5,000 pairs of shoes that the factory in Vietnam hasn't built yet because they ran out of rubber.

With an integrated ERP:

Sales enters the order in New York.

Manufacturing sees the demand instantly.

Inventory automatically checks for rubber. It sees a shortage.

Procurement is automatically triggered to buy rubber.

Finance instantly records the liability for the rubber purchase and projects the revenue from the sale.

Everyone acts in unison. There is one version of the truth.

3. Enterprise Performance Management (EPM)

The Strategic Compass

While the ERP manages the "day-to-day" operations, Enterprise Performance Management (EPM) helps management decide "what to do next."

EPM is often a layer of software that sits on top of the ERP. It is used for planning, budgeting, forecasting, and reporting. It is where the Management Accountant spends most of their time analyzing data to drive strategy.

The Difference Between ERP and EPM

ERP is transactional. It focuses on the past and present (What happened? What is happening?).

EPM is analytical. It focuses on the future (What should happen? How do we get there?).

Key Components of EPM

Planning, Budgeting, and Forecasting: Creating the annual budget and updating it with rolling forecasts.

Financial Consolidation: Combining the financial results of multiple subsidiaries into one parent view (crucial for multinational firms).

profitability Analysis: determining which products, customers, or regions are actually making money.

The 2026 Evolution: Agility and AI

In 2026, the annual static budget is dead. Business moves too fast. EPM systems now enable "Continuous Planning."

Scenario Modeling: "What if inflation hits 5%?" "What if a supplier goes bankrupt?" EPM systems allow CMAs to run these scenarios in minutes, not days.

Machine Learning Forecasting: Instead of humans guessing next month's sales, the EPM analyzes 5 years of history, weather patterns, and economic indicators to predict sales with high accuracy.

Visual Storytelling: EPMs output data into dynamic dashboards, not boring spreadsheets. This helps the CMA explain the numbers to non-financial executives.

Real-World Example: The Rolling Forecast

A retail chain uses EPM. Traditionally, they set a budget in January and stuck to it.

In 2026, they use a Rolling Forecast. Every month, the EPM system ingests the actual sales data from the ERP. It then uses AI to re-calculate the forecast for the next 12 months. If sales are trending down, the EPM highlights this immediately. The CFO can cut spending in Q3 because the system warned them in Q1. The strategy adjusts in real-time.

Hypothetical Financial Transaction & Problem Solving

To demonstrate how these systems interact, let's look at a complex manufacturing scenario involving a CMA in the year 2026.

The Scenario: "The Ghost Inventory"

Company: Apex Solar, a manufacturer of high-tech solar panels. Systems: They use an integrated Cloud ERP with a specialized EPM module for cost analysis.

The Transaction: On October 12, 2026, Apex Solar's procurement team orders 10,000 units of "silicon wafers" from a supplier in South Korea. The cost is $50 per unit.

Total Cost: $500,000.

Terms: FOB Shipping Point (Apex owns the goods once they leave the supplier).

The Data Flow:

ERP Supply Chain Module: Records the Purchase Order (PO).

ERP Logistics Module: Updates status to "In Transit" when goods leave Korea.

AIS/Finance Module: Should record the Inventory (asset) and Accounts Payable (liability).

The Problem

At month-end (October 31), the EPM Dashboard shows a massive dip in "Gross Margin." The CMA investigates.

The EPM shows that the Cost of Goods Sold (COGS) is normal, but the Inventory Turnover Ratio has plummeted.

Upon digging into the ERP, the CMA finds a discrepancy:

The Logistics Module shows the silicon wafers are still on a boat in the Pacific Ocean.

The Finance Module (AIS) has not recorded the inventory because the goods haven't physically arrived at the warehouse yet.

However, the legal title passed to Apex Solar when the goods left Korea (FOB Shipping Point).

Because the $500,000 asset is missing from the books, the Balance Sheet is understated. Furthermore, the automated production planning system (part of the ERP) thinks there are no wafers coming, so it has halted production scheduling, causing an efficiency variance.
The Solution

As the CMA, you must correct this using the systems.

Step 1: The Accounting Correction (AIS) You must intervene in the ERP Finance module. You create a "Goods in Transit" journal entry.

Debit: Inventory (Goods in Transit): $500,000

Credit: Accounts Payable: $500,000

This ensures the liability and the asset are recognized in the correct period (October), satisfying the "Matching Principle" and "Cut-off" assertions.

Step 2: The System Configuration (ERP) The problem was caused by a system trigger. The ERP was configured to recognize inventory only upon "Goods Receipt" (scanning at the warehouse door). You work with the IT specialists to update the ERP rule:

Logic Update: If Incoterms = "FOB Shipping Point," trigger financial recognition when the Logistics Module status changes to "Shipped," not "Received."

Step 3: Strategic Re-forecasting (EPM) Now that the system "sees" the inventory is on its way, you update the EPM production model.

The production schedule automatically updates to restart manufacturing on November 2nd (estimated arrival).

The EPM dashboard refreshes. The projected Gross Margin stabilizes because the production volume variance is eliminated.

Explanation of the Solution

This problem highlights the interdependence of systems. A simple accounting rule (FOB Shipping Point) was missed by the automated ERP configuration.

By manually correcting the AIS (the journal entry), re-configuring the ERP (the logic), and updating the EPM (the forecast), the CMA ensures accurate financial reporting and keeps the factory running efficiently.

Conclusion

For the 2026 Certified Management Accountant, technology is not just a tool; it is the environment in which we work.

AIS provides the data integrity and processes the high volume of transactions with automation.

ERP breaks down walls between departments, creating a single source of operational and financial truth.

EPM empowers the finance team to look forward, model the future, and guide the strategic direction of the company.

Understanding the flow of data from a raw invoice (AIS) through the operational chain (ERP) and finally into a strategic dashboard (EPM) is what separates a data entry clerk from a strategic business partner.

1. Data Policies and Procedures
The Constitution of Your Data Estate

If an organization were a country, Data Policies would be its constitution, and Data Procedures would be its laws. In 2026, we do not just write policies to satisfy auditors; we write them to enable safe speed.

A Data Policy is a high-level statement of intent. It outlines what must be done. For example, a policy might state: "All Customer Personally Identifiable Information (PII) must be encrypted at rest and in transit."

A Data Procedure is the tactical instruction manual. It explains how the policy is executed. It might say: "Use AES-256 encryption for database columns A, B, and C. Keys must be rotated every 90 days."
Key Policy Areas for 2026

The 2026 landscape introduces new complexities that standard policies from 2020 cannot handle.

AI Acceptable Use Policy: With Generative AI integrated into ERP systems (like NetSuite or SAP), employees might be tempted to paste sensitive financial forecasts into public chatbots to "summarize trends." A robust 2026 policy explicitly forbids inputting non-public financial data into public LLMs (Large Language Models) while establishing protocols for using private, enterprise-grade AI tools.

Data Sovereignty & Cross-Border Transfer: As global privacy laws fragment (GDPR in Europe, CCPA in California, and emerging laws in Asia), policies must dictate where data can physically reside. You cannot simply store German payroll data on a server in Texas without specific legal frameworks in place.

Ethical Data Usage (ESG Focus): Policies now extend to ethics. Just because we can collect data on employee keystrokes to measure productivity, should we? 2026 governance demands a "Privacy by Design" policy where data minimization is the default—we only collect what is strictly necessary for the business purpose.

Verifiable Example: Consider the regulatory fines faced by major tech firms in the early 2020s for mishandling user data. These were often not failures of technology (the encryption worked), but failures of policy—engineers had access to data they didn't need, violating the principle of "Least Privilege."

2. Life Cycle of Data
From Cradle to Grave (and Rebirth)

Data has a heartbeat. It is born, it matures, it ages, and eventually, it must die. Understanding the Data Life Cycle is critical for cost management and legal compliance. Hoarding data "just in case" is now a toxic asset due to storage costs and litigation risks.

The 5 Stages of the 2026 Data Life Cycle

Creation/Capture: Data enters the system. In 2026, this is rarely manual entry. It is captured via IoT sensors on inventory, OCR (Optical Character Recognition) scanning of invoices, or API feeds from bank accounts.

The 2026 Challenge: Metadata tagging. If data isn't tagged with its sensitivity level (e.g., "Confidential," "Public") the moment it is created, it is effectively unmanageable.

Storage & Maintenance: Data is housed in databases, data lakes, or the cloud. The focus here is on Availability and Integrity.

Trend: The shift to "Green Storage." Companies are under pressure to reduce their carbon footprint. Storing petabytes of duplicate data consumes massive electricity. Efficient storage is now an ESG metric.

Usage: This is where value is extracted. Data is fed into dashboards, financial models, and AI algorithms.

Governance Check: Who is using it? Usage logs must be immutable. If a Controller changes a reserve estimate, the system must record who changed it, when, and why.

Archival: Data is no longer actively used but must be kept for regulatory reasons (e.g., the IRS requires 7 years for tax records).

Strategy: Move this data from expensive "hot" storage (fast access) to cheap "cold" storage (slower access).

Destruction (Purging): The most neglected stage. When the retention period expires, data must be securely destroyed.

2026 Reality: "Crypto-shredding" is the standard. Instead of overwriting the hard drive, you simply delete the encryption key. Without the key, the data is just random digital noise, effectively destroyed instantly.

3. Data Management

The Engine Room of Truth

Data Management is the technical execution of governance. It ensures that the data flowing through the organization is accurate, available, and consistent. For the CMA, this circles back to one concept: The Single Source of Truth.

Master Data Management (MDM)

Imagine a scenario where the Sales department lists a client as "Acme Corp" while the Billing department lists them as "Acme Corporation Inc." To the computer, these are two different companies. This creates chaos in credit limits and revenue recognition.

MDM Solution: Governance creates a "Golden Record"—a single, master reference for every customer, product, and vendor. All other systems must sync to this master list.

Data Quality Dimensions

In 2026, we measure data quality like we measure inventory quality. We look for:

Accuracy: Does the data reflect reality? (e.g., Is the inventory count in SAP the same as the count in the warehouse?)

Completeness: Is any data missing? (e.g., A vendor record without a tax ID is incomplete).

Timeliness: Is the data available when needed? Real-time reporting requires real-time data.

Consistency: Is the data the same across all platforms?

Data Stewardship

This is the human element. A Data Steward is not an IT person; they are usually a business user (like a Senior Accountant) responsible for the quality of a specific data set.

Example: The Controller is the Data Steward for the General Ledger. The Head of HR is the Data Steward for Employee Records. They own the definitions and the quality, while IT owns the infrastructure.

4. Controls Against Security Breaches
The Zero Trust Architecture

The old model of security was like a castle: a moat (firewall) on the outside, but once you crossed the moat, you were trusted. This model is dead.

The 2026 standard is Zero Trust. The premise is simple: "Never trust, always verify." Even if a user is inside the network, they cannot access the Payroll folder without verifying their identity again.
Key Controls for Finance Professionals

Multi-Factor Authentication (MFA): This is non-negotiable. Passwords alone are obsolete. Accessing financial systems requires a password plus a biometric scan (fingerprint/face) or a hardware token.

Encryption:

At Rest: Data stored on the disk is encrypted. If a thief steals the physical server, they cannot read the data.

In Transit: Data moving between the browser and the server is encrypted (TLS 1.3).

Role-Based Access Control (RBAC): Users are assigned access based on their job role, not their name. If a Junior Accountant is promoted to Manager, their access rights automatically update based on the new role.

Data Loss Prevention (DLP): These are automated tools that monitor outgoing traffic. If a user tries to email a spreadsheet containing 1,000 credit card numbers to a personal Gmail account, the DLP system instantly blocks the email and alerts the security team.

Hypothetical Financial Transaction & Problem Solving Scenario: The "Phantom" Vendor

Date: February 14, 2026 Context: GlobalTech Solutions, a mid-sized manufacturing firm, uses an AI-driven Accounts Payable (AP) system.

The Transaction: An invoice arrives via email for $48,500 from a vendor named "Apex Consulting Services." The AI system scans the PDF, matches the Purchase Order (PO) number to an approved PO in the system, and initiates a wire transfer draft.

The Problem: The PO exists and the amount matches. However, the Bank Account Number on the invoice is different from the one in the Master Data record for Apex Consulting. The AI flags this as a "Low Confidence" match but, due to a recent configuration change to speed up processing, the system is set to auto-approve matches if the PO and Amount align perfectly. The payment is scheduled for release in 2 hours.

Applying Data Governance to Solve the Problem

If this transaction goes through, GlobalTech loses $48,500 to a fraudster who spoofed the vendor's invoice (a classic Business Email Compromise attack). Here is how the Governance framework intercedes:

Control Activation (Automated Policy): A strict Data Validation Rule embedded in the governance framework triggers immediately. The rule states: "Any change in vendor banking details requires secondary manual approval."

Even though the AI "approved" the invoice matching, the payment execution is blocked because the beneficiary data (bank account) does not match the Master Data.

Incident Response (Data Stewardship): The system generates a "Data Integrity Alert" sent to the AP Manager (Data Steward).

The Alert: "Discrepancy detected in Vendor Master Data. Invoice Bank Account [Ending 9988] does not match Master Record [Ending 1122]."

Resolution Procedure: The AP Manager follows the Verification Procedure:

Do not email the vendor (their email might be compromised).

Call the vendor using the phone number on file in the Master Record (not the one on the suspicious invoice).

Outcome: The AP Manager calls Apex Consulting. They confirm they did not change their bank account. The invoice is identified as fraudulent.

The transaction is cancelled.

The security team is notified to blacklist the sender's email domain.

Governance Update: The AI configuration is rolled back. The "auto-approve" threshold is raised, ensuring that any data mismatch, no matter how small, triggers a human review.

Conclusion

In this scenario, technology (AI) almost caused a disaster, but Data Governance (the Master Data rule and the Validation Control) saved the company.

For the CMA of 2026, understanding the debits and credits is not enough. You must understand the data flows that create them. Governance is the assurance that your financial statements are not just balanced, but true.

A. System Development Life Cycle (SDLC) in Finance

The System Development Life Cycle (SDLC) is the structured framework used to build, maintain, and replace information systems. In the context of 2026 finance, this is no longer just about installing accounting software; it is about deploying agile, cloud-native financial ecosystems that can adapt to market changes instantly.

1. Planning and Requirement Analysis

This is the foundational phase where the "why" and "what" are established. In modern finance, this involves identifying inefficiencies in current workflows and defining the ROI of a new system. It is critical to gather input from all stakeholders, not just the IT department.

Example: A global retail company decides to upgrade its legacy ERP system because it takes five days to close the books at month-end. They define a requirement: the new system must reduce closing time to 4 hours using real-time data processing.

2. Design and Prototyping

Once requirements are clear, the system architecture is designed. This includes database design, user interface (UI) design, and defining how data will flow between modules (e.g., Accounts Payable to General Ledger). In 2026, "Low-Code" platforms allow finance professionals to participate in this design phase without deep coding knowledge.

Example: A fintech startup designs a new mobile invoicing app. Instead of writing code from scratch, they use a drag-and-drop interface to create a prototype where the finance team can visually test the "Submit Invoice" button and see if it correctly triggers an approval workflow.

3. Development (Build)

This is where the actual coding or configuration takes place. Modern SDLC favors "Agile" development over the traditional "Waterfall" method. This means building in small increments or "sprints" to release usable features quickly rather than waiting years for a finished product.

Example: A bank developing a credit risk algorithm breaks the project into two-week sprints. In the first sprint, they build the data ingestion module. In the second sprint, they build the scoring logic. This allows the risk managers to test and give feedback on the data module before the whole system is finished.

4. Testing

Before going live, the system must be rigorously tested for bugs, security vulnerabilities, and accuracy. In finance, accuracy is non-negotiable. Testing involves Unit Testing (testing individual components) and User Acceptance Testing (UAT), where actual accountants use the system to verify it works as intended.

Example: During UAT for a new payroll system, the payroll manager runs a parallel test. She processes the December payroll in both the old system and the new system. She finds a $0.05 discrepancy in tax calculations in the new system, which developers must fix before launch.

5. Deployment (Implementation)

This is the "Go Live" moment. Strategies vary: "Big Bang" (switching everything at once) or "Phased" (rolling out module by module). In 2026, deployment is often continuous, with updates pushed to the cloud automatically without downtime.

Example: A multinational corporation chooses a "Phased" deployment for its new expense management software. They launch it in their UK office first. After one month of smooth operations and positive feedback, they deploy it to the US and Asian offices.

6. Maintenance and Evolution

The lifecycle does not end at deployment. Systems need patching, updates, and optimization. In an AI-driven world, "maintenance" also means retraining machine learning models to ensure they stay accurate as market conditions change.

Example: An investment firm uses an AI bot to read market news. Six months after deployment, the bot starts misinterpreting sarcasm in tweets. The maintenance team retrains the AI model with new linguistic data to improve its sentiment analysis accuracy.

B. Process Automation

Process automation involves using technology to execute recurring tasks where manual effort can be replaced. By 2026, we are moving beyond simple automation into "Hyperautomation"—a state where AI and machine learning actively make decisions within the automated process.

1. Robotic Process Automation (RPA)

RPA uses software "bots" to mimic human actions on a computer. These bots are perfect for high-volume, repetitive tasks that follow strict rules. They do not "think"; they just follow instructions. They are the digital workforce of the finance department.

Example: A telecommunications company receives 5,000 invoices a day via email. Instead of humans downloading and typing data, an RPA bot opens every email, downloads the PDF, reads the invoice number and amount, and types it into the SAP system 24/7 without taking a break.

2. Intelligent Process Automation (IPA)

IPA combines RPA with Artificial Intelligence (AI). While RPA handles the "doing," AI handles the "thinking." IPA can process unstructured data like messy emails, scanned images, or handwriting, which traditional RPA cannot handle.

Example: A mortgage lender uses IPA to process loan applications. The RPA bot collects the documents. The AI component reads the scanned tax returns (even if they are wrinkled or handwritten), extracts the income figures, and determines if the borrower qualifies based on complex risk policies.

3. Hyperautomation

Hyperautomation is the strategic orchestration of various technologies (RPA, AI, Process Mining) to automate as many business and IT processes as possible. It creates a "digital twin" of the organization where processes are continuously monitored and optimized by the system itself.

Example: A logistics firm uses hyperautomation for its supply chain finance. If a shipment is delayed due to weather (detected by IoT sensors), the system automatically updates the cash flow forecast, notifies the CFO of the potential revenue dip, and halts payments to non-critical vendors to preserve cash—all without human intervention.

4. Benefits of Automation in Finance

The primary benefits are speed, accuracy, and cost reduction. But the 2026 perspective focuses on "Talent Elevation." When bots do the boring work, finance professionals can focus on strategic analysis and business partnering.

Example: By automating the bank reconciliation process, a junior accountant saves 15 hours a week. She uses this freed-up time to analyze sales trends and presents a report to the marketing director that helps launch a profitable new product line.

C. Innovative Applications

Innovative applications refer to the cutting-edge technologies that are redefining the boundaries of what is possible in finance. In 2026, these are no longer experimental; they are mainstream drivers of competitive advantage.

1. Blockchain and Distributed Ledger Technology (DLT)

Blockchain is a shared, immutable ledger that facilitates the process of recording transactions and tracking assets in a business network. In finance, it creates "Smart Contracts"—self-executing contracts with the terms directly written into code. This eliminates the need for intermediaries like banks or lawyers for many transactions.

Example: A coffee chain uses blockchain to pay Ethiopian farmers. When the shipment arrives at the US port and is scanned, a Smart Contract automatically releases payment to the farmers' digital wallets instantly. There are no wire fees, no delays, and complete transparency on the price paid.

2. Cloud Computing and SaaS

Cloud computing delivers computing services—servers, storage, databases, networking, software—over the Internet ("the cloud"). For finance, this means data is accessible from anywhere, fostering remote work and real-time collaboration. It shifts IT costs from CapEx (buying servers) to OpEx (monthly subscriptions).

Example: During a merger, Company A and Company B need to consolidate financial statements. Because both use a cloud-based ERP (like Oracle NetSuite), they can grant access to each other's data instantly. They complete the financial integration in weeks rather than the months it would take to physically merge server rooms.

3. The Internet of Things (IoT)

IoT refers to the network of physical objects—"things"—embedded with sensors and software to exchange data. In finance, IoT provides real-time data that improves asset tracking, inventory management, and risk assessment.

Example: An insurance company offers "Usage-Based Insurance" for a fleet of delivery trucks. IoT sensors in the trucks track speed, braking, and mileage. The finance system calculates the insurance premium monthly based on actual driving behavior. Safe driving results in a lower bill, directly impacting the company's P&L.

4. Big Data and Predictive Analytics

Finance generates massive amounts of data. innovative applications use Big Data tools to analyze this information to predict future trends. This moves finance from "descriptive" (what happened?) to "predictive" (what will happen?) and "prescriptive" (how can we make it happen?).

Example: A fashion retailer analyzes weather patterns, social media trends, and historical sales data. The system predicts that yellow raincoats will be a trend in October. The finance team approves the budget to stock up on inventory in August, ensuring they meet demand and maximize revenue.

Hypothetical Financial Transaction & Problem Solving

The Scenario: The "Smart" Supply Chain Transaction

Context: Imagine "AutoTech 2026," a manufacturer of electric vehicle parts. They utilize a fully integrated Technology-Enabled Finance ecosystem involving Blockchain, IoT, and AI-driven Process Automation.

The Transaction: AutoTech orders 1,000 lithium batteries from a supplier in South Korea.

Smart Contract (Blockchain): The purchase order is a Smart Contract. It states: "Release 30% payment upon shipment. Release remaining 70% when goods arrive at the California warehouse only if the temperature of the container never exceeded 25°C."

IoT Monitoring: The shipping container has IoT sensors tracking location and temperature every minute.

Process Automation: The ERP system at AutoTech is watching the blockchain for updates to trigger inventory entries automatically.

The Problem: The shipment arrives in California. The IoT sensor data uploads to the blockchain. However, the Smart Contract fails to execute the final 70% payment. The supplier is angry and halts future shipments, threatening AutoTech's production line. The finance team sees the inventory physically in the warehouse, but the system refuses to pay.

Investigation: The Finance Systems Analyst investigates. They look at the IoT data log. It shows that for 15 minutes during transit across the Pacific, the temperature sensor reported 150°C. This is physically impossible for the container without it being on fire (which it wasn't). The Smart Contract logic was rigid: "If Temp > 25°C, Block Payment."

The Solution:

Step 1: Diagnose the Root Cause (Data Anomaly) The analyst identifies that the IoT sensor malfunctioned briefly, sending a "glitch" reading of 150°C. This is a "False Positive" data error. The automation (Smart Contract) worked correctly based on its code, but the real-world outcome was wrong.

Step 2: Manual Override & Settlement (Human Intervention) The CMA (Certified Management Accountant) on duty reviews the physical condition of the batteries. They test a sample; the batteries are perfect. The CMA authorizes a manual "override" transaction outside the Smart Contract to wire the 70% payment immediately to the supplier to restore the relationship.

Step 3: System Correction (SDLC Update) The Finance team logs a ticket for the IT developers.

Requirement: The Smart Contract logic needs to be "smarter" to ignore outliers.

Design/Build: The developers update the code to use an "Average Temperature over 1 hour" rather than a single instant reading, or to flag readings above 60°C as "Sensor Error" rather than "Temperature Breach."

Test: They simulate a sensor glitch in a test environment. The new code ignores the glitch and approves the payment.

Deploy: The updated Smart Contract is deployed for the next shipment.

Explanation: This scenario illustrates that while Process Automation and Blockchain provide speed and trust, they lack "common sense." SDLC was required to fix the system flaw. The human finance professional (CMA) was essential to bridge the gap between rigid code and business reality, solving the immediate liquidity crisis and guiding the technological improvement.

4a. Business Intelligence (BI)

The Concept

Business Intelligence (BI) is the technology-driven process for analyzing data and delivering actionable information that helps executives, managers, and workers make informed business decisions. In the context of 2026, BI has evolved from static, monthly PDF reports to dynamic, real-time ecosystems.

Think of BI as the "rear-view mirror" with a GPS overlay. It tells you exactly where you have been and what is happening right now, using historical data to optimize current performance.

The Evolution in Management Accounting

Traditionally, a management accountant might spend a week compiling a variance report. By 2026, BI tools (like advanced versions of Microsoft Power BI, Tableau, or Qlik) automate this ingestion. The focus is now on Self-Service BI. This means finance professionals build the architecture that allows operational managers to query data themselves without waiting for IT.

Key Components of Modern BI

Data Warehousing: The central repository where data from different sources (sales, payroll, inventory) is consolidated.

ETL (Extract, Transform, Load): The plumbing that moves data from source to warehouse, cleaning it along the way.

Dashboards: The user interface that displays KPIs (Key Performance Indicators) visually.

Example: Consider a retail clothing chain. A regional manager uses a BI dashboard on their tablet. Instead of waiting for the end-of-month P&L, they see sales data updated every 15 minutes. They notice that "Winter Coats" are selling 40% slower than anticipated in the Northeast region. The BI tool highlights this variance in red. The manager immediately clicks a button to apply a 15% discount to move inventory, a decision made in minutes rather than weeks.

2026 Trends in BI

Natural Language Querying (NLQ): You no longer need to know SQL code. You simply type, "Show me gross margin by product line for Q3 compared to last year," and the BI tool generates the chart.

Embedded BI: Analytics are no longer in a separate app; they are embedded directly into the ERP (Enterprise Resource Planning) systems where accountants work daily.

4b. Data Mining
The Concept

If BI is looking at the fruit on the tree, Data Mining is examining the soil to understand why the fruit grew that way. It is the process of discovering patterns, correlations, and anomalies within large datasets to predict outcomes.

Data mining relies heavily on statistics, artificial intelligence, and machine learning. For the CMA, this is about risk management and finding hidden value.
Core Techniques

Clustering: Grouping data points that are similar.

Usage: Segmenting customers based on payment history to adjust credit terms.

Regression Analysis: Determining relationships between variables.

Usage: Determining how much utility costs rise for every degree drop in temperature.

Association Rule Learning: finding interesting relations between variables.

Usage: The classic "Market Basket Analysis." If a client buys a specialized machine, they are 80% likely to buy the extended warranty.

The Role of "Big Data"

By 2026, "Big Data" isn't just a buzzword; it's the standard. Financial data is structured (ledgers, spreadsheets), but data mining now scrapes unstructured data—emails, social media sentiment, and satellite imagery—to inform financial models.

Example: A large insurance company suspects fraudulent claims. Human auditors cannot review 100,000 claims manually. They use data mining algorithms to scan for "red flag" patterns—perhaps a specific doctor ID appearing on claims from three different cities on the same day. The system flags these anomalies for human review. This is data mining protecting the bottom line.

4c. Types of Data Analytics

The industry standard model for analytics is a hierarchy of value. As a CMA, you must move your organization from

the bottom of the ladder (Descriptive) to the top (Prescriptive).
1. Descriptive Analytics (What happened?)

This is the foundation. It summarizes raw data to make it interpretable.

Nature: Hindsight.

Tools: Basic financial statements, variance analysis, pie charts.

CMA Application: "Sales revenue for January was $100,000, which is down 5% from December."

2. Diagnostic Analytics (Why did it happen?)

This digs into the root cause. It involves drilling down, data discovery, and correlations.

Nature: Insight.

Tools: Drill-down dashboards, correlation matrices.

CMA Application: "Sales were down because the primary supplier for Product X was delayed, causing stockouts."

3. Predictive Analytics (What will happen?)

This uses statistical models and forecasting techniques to understand the future. This is where the CMA adds immense strategic value.

Nature: Foresight.

Tools: Regression models, machine learning forecasting.

CMA Application: "Based on current supply chain trends and seasonality, we predict sales will rebound by 10% in February, provided inventory arrives by the 5th."

4. Prescriptive Analytics (How can we make it happen?)

The pinnacle of analytics. It suggests decision options to take advantage of a future opportunity or mitigate a future risk.

Nature: Optimization.

Tools: AI simulation, optimization algorithms.

CMA Application: "To ensure the February rebound, the system recommends we switch 30% of our orders to Supplier B, even though they are slightly more expensive, to guarantee delivery speed."

Example: An airline uses all four types.

Descriptive: The flight was delayed 30 mins.

Diagnostic: It was delayed because of a mechanical check.

Predictive: This specific part is likely to fail every 5,000 flight hours.

Prescriptive: Automatically schedule maintenance for this aircraft at 4,800 hours to prevent a delay next time.

4d. Data Visualization

The Concept

Data visualization is the graphic representation of data. It involves producing images that communicate relationships among the represented data to viewers. For the 2026 CMA, being a "data storyteller" is a required soft skill. You cannot just present a spreadsheet; you must present a narrative.

Principles of Effective Visualization

Clarity over Beauty: Avoid "chart junk" (3D effects, excessive shadows) that distracts from the numbers.

Context: A number without context is meaningless. Always show comparisons (vs. Budget, vs. Last Year, vs. Competitors).

Hierarchy: The most important information should be in the top left (where the eye starts).

Common Visuals in Finance

Waterfall Charts: perfect for showing how you got from a starting cash balance to an ending balance (Revenue -> Cost of Goods -> Opex -> Net Income).

Heat Maps: Excellent for risk assessment (High probability/High impact risks show in bright red).

Bullet Charts: The best replacement for gauges/speedometers to show progress toward a target.

Example: A CFO is presenting to the Board of Directors. Instead of a 50-page deck of tables, she presents a single interactive dashboard. It features a Waterfall Chart showing exactly where EBITDA leaked this quarter. When a board member asks about "Marketing Spend," she hovers over that bar, and it expands to show the detail. The visualization answers the question instantly, building trust and authority.

Hypothetical Financial Scenario & Problem Solving

To demonstrate the practical application of these concepts for the 2026 CMA, let us look at a specific hypothetical scenario.
The Scenario: EcoLogistics Inc.

EcoLogistics Inc. is a mid-sized logistics company that manages a fleet of 500 electric delivery trucks. They are facing a squeeze on margins.

The Problem: Maintenance costs are rising unpredictably, and vehicle downtime is causing missed delivery SLAs (Service Level Agreements), resulting in penalties.

The Goal: Reduce maintenance costs by 15% and cut downtime by 20%.

The management accounting team decides to implement a Prescriptive Analytics solution using data from the trucks' IoT (Internet of Things) sensors.
The Transaction/Event

On October 12, 2026, the system flags Truck #402.

Descriptive Data: The truck's battery temperature is running 4% higher than average.

Predictive Model: The algorithm predicts a 92% probability of battery failure within the next 200 miles.

Financial Implication:

Cost of Reactive Repair (Breakdown on road): Towing ($500) + Emergency Part Premium ($1,200) + SLA Penalty ($800) + Driver Overtime ($200) = $2,700.

Cost of Prescriptive Maintenance (Scheduled now): Standard Part ($1,000) + Standard Labor ($300) = $1,300.

The Problem

Calculate the Net Financial Benefit of the analytics system for this single event, and project the ROI (Return on Investment) for the year if the system costs $50,000 annually to license and this event occurs 100 times a year across the fleet.

The Solution

Step 1: Calculate Cost Avoidance per Event We compare the cost of doing nothing (Reactive) vs. acting on the data (Prescriptive).

CostReactive=$2,700
CostPrescriptive=$1,300
Savings=CostReactive−CostPrescriptive
Savings=$2,700−$1,300=$1,400

Step 2: Annualize the Savings The scenario states this type of failure is predicted and prevented 100 times per year.

Total_Annual_Savings=$1,400×100=$140,000

Step 3: Calculate ROI The cost of the analytics software license is $50,000.

ROI=Cost_of_InvestmentNet_Profit×100
Net_Profit=Total_Annual_Savings−License_Cost
Net_Profit=$140,000−$50,000=$90,000
ROI=$50,000$90,000×100=180%

Explanation: By utilizing Prescriptive Analytics, EcoLogistics Inc. not only solves the operational issue of vehicle downtime but generates a massive financial return. The management accountant captures this value not by fixing the truck, but by validating the investment in the data software. This is the essence of the 2026 CMA role: validating technology investments through rigorous financial analysis.

Closing Thoughts

Data analytics is no longer a "nice-to-have" skill for accountants; it is the license to operate. Whether it is using Business Intelligence to monitor real-time cash flow, Data Mining to detect fraud, or Visualization to persuade the Board, the tools described above are what separate the bookkeeper of the past from the strategic financial leader of the future.

About Author

Azhar ul Haque Sario is a bestselling author and data scientist with a remarkable record of achievement. This Cambridge alumnus brings a wealth of knowledge to his work, holding an MBA (SZABIST), ACCA (Knowledge Level - FTMS College Malaysia and London College of Accountancy, London), BBA, and several Google certifications, including specializations in Google Data Analytics, Google Digital Marketing & E-commerce, and Google Project Management.

With ten years of business experience, Azhar combines practical expertise with his impressive academic background to craft insightful books. His prolific writing has resulted in an astounding 2810 published titles, earning him the record for the maximum Kindle editions and paperback books published by an individual author in one year, awarded by Asia Books of Records in 2024.

ORCID: https://orcid.org/0009-0004-8629-830X
Azhar.sario@hotmail.co.uk
https://www.linkedin.com/in/azharulhaquesario/

www.ingramcontent.com/pod-product-compliance
Lightning Source LLC
Chambersburg PA
CBHW031343230926
51848CB00002B/356